Critical Interruptions

CRITICAL INTERRUPTIONS

*New Left Perspectives
on Herbert Marcuse*

Edited by Paul Breines

Herder and Herder

1972

HERDER AND HERDER

232 Madison Avenue, New York 10016

ISBN 665–00018–9

Library of Congress Catalog Card Number: 72–110786

Contents

CONTENTS

vi

THIS BOOK IS DEDICATED TO

THEODOR W. ADORNO

AND

HO CHI MINH

Editor's Notes

Herbert Marcuse's leap from the hinterlands of heretical and *avant-garde* Marxian theory to celebrity status as the primal father of the global revolt of students and youth is a sign, as it were, of the times. Almost overnight the unknown dialectician became, in *Fortune*'s phrase, the "improbable guru of surrealistic politics" and simultaneously evoked the wrath of authorities and authoritarians everywhere. Indeed, it is one of the unique achievements of Marcuse's work that it has united California's right-wing elders, *Pravda,* liberals such as Irving Howe and Nathan Glazer, the French Communist Party, and, most recently, the Pope in a single chorus of reprobation against the supposed pied piper who has corrupted the minds, morals, and manners of the young. Like all theories of the outside agitator, the Marcuse guru-myth is geared to cover up the inside agitators: repressive-bureaucratic capitalism and socialism themselves. If Marcuse's critique of modern society, and his perspectives on the "non-repressive civilization" which this society is mobilized against, have seized a part of the masses, they have done so because his critique and vision were already in the air, written there by repressive civilization.

The sticky ideological web that now clings to Marcuse's name and work has extended to limits that are truly out of sight. These limits reach from the sublime:

(*Le Monde,* May 20, 1969:) MARCUSE IS OBJECTIVELY OUR ALLY, declares the Communist philosopher, Georgy Lukács. "In spite of their errors, Marcuse and Bloch [Ernst Bloch, a German maverick Marxian philosopher] are objectively our allies and, in my opinion, one cannot deny that they are authentic enemies of imperialism," declared the Hungarian philosopher, Georgy Lukács, in a long interview accorded *Kortars,* a monthly journal of Hungarian writers. M. Lukács nevertheless expressed the view that all books need not be placed in all hands. In my opinion, "it is not necessary that the works of Marquis de Sade be translated into Hungarian . . . it would be normal for de Sade's books to be at the disposal of sociologists, but I would not want them disseminated among the young students . . ."

to the insidious, as in the article published by the Progressive Labor Party in this country "proving" that Marcuse has been an active CIA agent and that the function of his books and recent travels has been to aid the international ruling class in its suppression of the revolts of students and workers.[1] What gives this particular bit of Marcuseana its significance is the fact that the Progressive Labor Party has of late been successful in recruiting and influencing relatively large numbers within the New Left, and the fact that as of Fall 1969, PLP's charges against Marcuse have not been openly repudiated (with one isolated exception[2])

---

[1] "Marcuse: Cop-out or Cop?", *Progressive Labor,* 6:6 (February, 1969), 61–66.

[2] See the pamphlet by Murray Bookchin, *Listen, Marxist!* (New York: Anarchos, 1969), esp. p. 23. I consider this pamphlet as a whole to be

by any New Left publications or statements in this country.

A similar "critique" of Marcuse was recently presented in West Germany. There, however, a direct response from associates of the German *SDS* and "extra-parliamentary opposition" was immediately forthcoming. It is a response with which the contributors to the present book are in complete accord:

For years the New Left has struggled against the traditional party bureaucracies and authoritarian welfare-states to liberate the initiatives of solidarity and the political interests of the people. In this struggle it has refused to base itself on a closed and obligatory theory or an air-tight strategy. It thus contradicts its own principles and goals when the desperately needed discussion within the Left is obstructed by the revival of the Stalinist practice of accusing representatives of deviating positions of being agents of enemy powers. Those who characterize Herbert Marcuse as a CIA agent or an agent of the bourgeoisie . . . have departed from the terrain on which the New Left is working. These denunciations have nothing to do with the legitimate means of fractional struggles. Rather, they create an atmosphere in which finally no one is secure from suspicion, personal defamation, and moral assassination.

We declare our solidarity with Herbert Marcuse, who has been indispensable to the theory and practice of the New Left, and who has always been unequivocally in solidarity with the student movement and the social-revolutionary struggles of the Third World. We call on all socialists to resist those who take part in the attacks on Marcuse which reactionaries of all shades have set in motion. Such practices contradict all the interests of the New Left.[3]

---

an exemplary critique of many of the recent developments within the American New Left.

[3] The statement appeared in *Der Spiegel,* 31 (July 28, 1969), 13–14. Among the sixteen signers were: Rudi Dutschke, Erich Fired, Klaus Meschkat, Oskar Negt, Reimut Reiche.

The terms in which we ourselves consider Marcuse "indispensable to the theory and practice of the New Left" are elaborated in the following pages. The essays collected here speak well enough for themselves—in numerous instances they speak to and with one another;[4] in others, against each other. The theoretical and practical coherence of the book as a whole is left to the reader to trace, for the point around which the essays were originally conceived was at once too limited and too expansive to be the basis of a collective project that moved in a clearly unified direction. We agreed that Marcuse is a mind and a mind-bender in an era of officially administered and popularly endorsed mindlessness. His works *are* what they call for—a disruption of the somnambulism of everyday life and thought, a liberation of self, consciousness, and imagination from their entombment in the reified structures of advanced capitalist society. In this sense, we agreed too that Marcuse's work is the theoretical starting point of criticism of this society. (And in the same sense we are part of a larger corps of kindred spirits presently operating both above and beneath the surfaces.)

What each of the essays does from this point, how much further beyond it each one or all move, is not entirely for the contributors to judge. For the record, we do not all know each other and we came to Marcuse and his work in different ways. Several of us studied with him directly at Brandeis and/or the University of California at San Diego; others indirectly and from a distance through his books and essays. In one way or another each of us is part of the present movement of revolt against "one-dimensional" existence in general and America's advanced technics of destruction in particular. We hope that our book is a frac-

---

[4] In particular, the essays by Shierry Weber and Jeremy J. Shapiro emanate from an on-going discussion and collaborative focus.

tion as useful to the movement as Marcuse's own work has been.

In my work as editor I am deeply grateful to a number of comrades and friends for their spiritual, theoretical, and editorial help: Wini Breines, Jeremy Shapiro, Shierry Weber, Russell Jacoby, Barrie Thorne, Charlotte Nathanson, Elliott Eisenberg, and to Trude Bennett for typing assistance.

While this book was being put together, the movements for liberation from daily life in the American empire lost Ho Chi Minh and Theodor W. Adorno. Their deaths are additional reminder that "only the bad in history is irrevocable: the unrealized possibilities, the lost joys, death with and without due process—all that the rulers have done to the ruled. The rest stands always in danger" (Max Horkheimer). I chose to dedicate the book to them.

PAUL BREINES

Critical Interruptions

From Guru to Spectre:
Marcuse and the Implosion of the Movement

PAUL BREINES

Critiques and commentaries on Herbert Marcuse abound and they abound because his works got hooked up with the global student-youth revolt as have those of no other contemporary Western theorist. The sociology of this conjuncture of theory and practice—and in particular of the spectacular publicity, celebration, and deformation that has accompanied it—is only beginning, but several things are already clear. First, there is the evident fact that "the student movements which he [Marcuse] neither predicted nor inspired, but which, through their primarily cultural and moral demands (secondarily, and in certain countries, economic demands), found in his works and ultimately *in his works alone* the theoretical formulation of their problems and aspirations."[1] Second, there is the apparently mystical dimension to the situation: "it is obvious that most students who cite or proclaim Marcuse ignore the bulk of his writings and thought." Whether, on this question, it is sufficient to say that "they are right in doing so [for]

[1] Lucien Goldmann, "La Pensée de Herbert Marcuse," *La Nef*, 36 (January–March, 1969), 56. Emphasis in original.

1

social life has its own logic and everywhere po·sesses means of disseminating thought other than direct reading and the mass media,"[2] is open to question, but this cannot be taken up in detail here. Third, given the uniquely pervasive character of his impact, it is nevertheless true that "anyone who considers Marcuse the theorist of the Movement understands neither Marcuse nor the Movement." Yet at the same time it does not follow that Marcuse was "tacked onto the Movement" by the media and the myth-gurus, even though the Madison Avenue-Baroque extremes to which the guru-mythology has been carried often gives this impression.[3]

Rather, and fourth, the extent to which Marcuse has been made into a publicity stunt is a moment in the larger fact that *both* his work and the Movement are subject to the processes of commodification, reification, and "one-dimensionalization" which they revolted against in the first place. This development exemplifies the political-technological phenomenon noted some thirty years ago by Marcuse's friend, Walter Benjamin: "the bourgeois publication and production apparatus can assimilate and even publicize an astonishing number of revolutionary themes without thereby throwing into question either its own basis or the basis of the class that controls it."[4] The virtually boundless character achieved by this assimilative capacity today is well enough known and need not be summarized in any detail. It is well known not only through Marcuse's own critique of it but, as suggested above, through the subsumption of his critique in it. Thus an ad such as

[2] *Ibid.,* fn.

[3] René Viénet, *Enragés et Situationistes dans le mouvement des occupations* (Paris: Gallimard, 1968), 153.

[4] Walter Benjamin, *Versuche über Brecht* (Frankfurt-Main: Suhrkamp, 1966), 105.

2

"Don't be a One-Dimensional Man, Spray on Lotion-X" hardly seems particularly far out, since in essence it has already appeared on the scene. Developments such as this are, in turn, part of the fact that in advanced industrial society everyone is reduced to the mode of spectator at the show of his own alienated activity. The appearance of the "Marcuse spectacle" is, then, an issue worthy of analysis in itself: it opens up critical study of the dialectics of cultural revolution and forces one to ask the extent to which the assimilation and integration of Marcuse—as well as of the New Left, the Hippies, youth culture—by the ruling apparatus may be part of the emerging disintegration of the apparatus.

Useful as this might be, the present essay will have a different though related focus, one made necessary by recent and fundamental shifts in the New Left Movement itself and therefore in the relationship between it and Marcuse's works. Specifically, among the New Left's supposedly more advanced, "political" sectors Marcuse's work is becoming an object of growing resentment, as it always has been for the traditional Marxist or Old Left. Two glimpses into what has been happening: during the mass upheaval in France in May 1968, the identity between many of his main theses and the revolutionary manifestoes and graffiti initiated a new wave of inane speculation on Marcuse as the prime mover of the *enragés*. But from amidst the hullabaloo came reports such as the following from a spokesman of one of the French Trotskyist organizations: at a mass meeting of students in early May a consensus was reached that "the student struggle could only be a part of the struggle for socialism; and the main social force in this struggle was the working class. No remarks of a Marcusean or similar type were

3

listened to."[5] Since our own focus will be on developments in the United States, it is irrelevant whether this report is mere sectarian wish-think or whether it is accurate in the French context: it adequately characterizes the bulk of meetings, writings, and general thinking within the New Left here during the past two years or so. The second glimpse: the charges, levelled by the Progressive Labor Party, that Marcuse is a CIA agent, are not merely psychotic. Nor does the fact that the charges have not been vehemently repudiated by the Movement suggest that the New Left *en masse* believes them. Rather the charges are a psychotic spin-off from an emerging consensus around the idea that the supposedly metapolitical, post-political, utopian, personal liberation, anti-working class stage in the Movement's development—with Marcuse being taken as one of the main symbols of this stage—must be exorcized and surpassed.

This shift away from Marcuse is evident not only in the U.S. but is "Western-wide"; and *in principle* a shift which carried the Movements' practical theory and conscious practice beyond both Marcuse and its own previous stages *could* be an unquestionable and vital advance. The whole point of Marcuse's work is that it be superseded on all levels, and numerous theorists within and close to the Movement have attempted to specify the lines which the practical and theoretical critique might follow.[6] While such

[5] Pierre Frank, "From a Student Upheaval Towards a Proletarian Socialist Revolution," in Tariq Ali, ed., *The New Revolutionaries: A Handbook of the International Radical Left* (New York: Morrow, 1969), 180.

[6] See among others: Paul Mattick, "The Limits of Integration," in K. H. Wolff and B. Moore, eds., *The Critical Spirit: Essays in Honor of Herbert Marcuse* (Boston: Beacon, 1967), 347–400; Peter Sedgewick, "Natural Science and Human Theory," *The Socialist Register, 1966* (London: Merlin, 1966), 163–192; the essays in Jürgen Habermas, ed., *Antworten auf Herbert Marcuse* (Frankfurt-Main: Suhrkamp,

analyses were appearing before it, the May 1968 explosion gave them additional impetus but also gave many a rather infantile undertone of "See, Gran'pa, you were wrong, the working class *is* revolutionary, look out there in the streets!" One of the most provocative and serious of these "post-May" criticisms is Henri Lefebvre's and the following excerpt may be taken as a valuable statement of the challenge:

If the movement of students and intellectuals enlarges a crevice, this means that the wall is cracking. And here we have an *action-critique* of Marcuse's thesis [that Advanced Industrial Society is closed and impervious to revolutionary transformation], at least as far as France and Europe are concerned. Since it can also be shown in other connections that current social phenomena do not fit in Marcuse's concepts and categories, this indicates that his analysis is inadequate. Theoretical criticism—the formulation of practice—will be continued, but on different ground. The question of acting "subjects," and of objects and projects (of the real and the possible) will be posed in new terms. And should knowledge become able to give form to spontaneity, the acceptable aspect of Marcuse's work will have been determined and delineated: that is, *its utopian function* during a certain period.[7]

Lefebvre's qualifications are as important as his proposition itself; together they establish the premises of the following pages. He first of all is correct in restricting himself to France and Europe. Second, he emphasizes that the acceptable aspect of Marcuse's work (which in Lefebvre's view is the argument in *Eros and Civilization* regarding the eroticization of existence which could result from a

---

1968); Pier Aldo Rovatti, "Marcuse and the 'Crisis of the European Sciences,'" *Telos*, 1:2 (Fall, 1968), 113–115; and the essay by Jeremy J. Shapiro in this book.

[7] Henri Lefebvre, *The Explosion: Marxism and the French Upheaval* (New York and London: Monthly Review, 1969), 31.

break with the present linkage of libido to production and consumption and the restriction of desire to the genital and procreative functions, as well as Marcuse's insights into the linkage of politics and eros in the student-youth revolt) will be delineated *if and when* knowledge becomes capable of giving form to spontaneity. Third, the surpassing of the utopian function of Marcuse's work and the stage of the Movement in the U.S. to which it corresponded is today being widely announced and it is the extent to which this may be true that we want to examine. Finally, we agree with Lefebvre that the wall is cracking and that a key cause as well as effect of this situation is the revolt of students, youth, and intellectuals: this is what gives the discussion its meaning.

Before proceeding it should be made clear that the Movement, above all in this country, has never been a "Marcusean" movement, and it would be silly to insist that it should have been or should be, whatever that might mean. Aside from the fact that no social movement springs from the head of a theorist, the New Left in this country has been the proud progeny of the isolation and insulation from dialectical social theory which has historically defined American intellectuals in general and Left intellectuals in particular. The situation within the German Movement, for example, where "the 'Frankfurt School' [Max Horkheimer, Marcuse, T. W. Adorno, *et al.*] has been very useful to the young intellectuals . . . for a whole generation of socialist students it was one of the most important starting points,"[8] hardly obtained here. But it is precisely within this built-in truncation that the structure of the links between Marcuse and the Movement here took shape: central among the new, liberatory needs generated

8 Wolfgang Abendroth, in Theo Pinkus, ed., *Gespräche mit Georg Lukács* (Hamburg: Rowohlt, 1967), 80.

by the student-youth revolt is the need for dialectical social theory.

Within this general structure Marcuse's thought has been a key component in the Movement's process of self-constitution and self-comprehension in more specific ways. These will be celebrated in somewhat greater detail below, but for the moment several aspects can be mentioned. Marcuse's analysis of "one-dimensional man" took hold within wide sections of the New Left because it corresponded to the *experience* of many in or entering the Movement: part of a generation began to perceive that it was living or was supposed to live a one-dimensional existence and could not tolerate it. Further, his analysis of the "new politics" established by advanced industrial society and the new type of opposition it necessitated went to the core of the New Left's situation and activity: the modern technics of production, consumption, administration, and destruction have issued in radically new modes of political-social domination, manipulation, and alienation (intricating the instinctual, sexual, cultural, and linguistic dimensions into society's self-reproductive process), and this requires that, if possible at all, political-economic revolution must be preceded and shaped by a radical and collective *self*-transformation of men and women—their consciousness, language, values, instincts, desires, needs. And the existing society's incorporation of phantasy, the imagination, the aesthetic into its system of hegemony and the "fantastic" liberatory possibilities created and blocked by the prevailing form of modern technology, makes essential the re-incorporation of phantasy, imagination, and aesthetics into critical theory and practice. Traversing these arguments is a perspective which originated with the "young Marx" and which the "young Marcuse" adopted as the fundament of his conception of revolution: the

7

abolition of private property in the means of production is the mere (and necessary) precondition of socialism and communism, whose *aim* is the liberation of men and society from subjugation to economic-political relationships as such.[9] This perspective has been implicitly and explicitly developed by Marcuse in all of his more recent works. And in these "Marcusean theses" the Movement glimpsed itself, its own self-consciousness.

Finally in this sketch, Marcuse's analysis (particularly several of his revisions of classical Marxian theory) included the argument that the industrial working class has been integrated into the ruling system—as a beneficiary of its productivity and as an active consumer of its commodities and "commodity way of life"—and no longer embodies the "vital need for revolution," but has become part of society's conservative, popular base. It is probably accurate to say that until recently the New Left by and large accepted this argument (which is not Marcuse's alone) or did not particularly care about it, but either way moved ahead on the assumption that the Movement was working in what Marcuse termed the "society without opposition." Thus, simultaneous with the publication of *One-Dimensional Man* (1964), Marcuse found in the Movement both an emerging practical refutation of some of his claims regarding the closed, oppositionless character of the ruling society, and an emerging realization of some of the utopian "political-erotic" concepts formulated in *Eros and Civilization* (1955), and he began to direct his own energies increasingly toward the New Left. By 1966–67

[9] See especially Marcuse's review of the first publication in German of Marx's "Economic and Philosophical Manuscripts" of 1844, "Neue Quellen zur Grundlegung des historischen Materialismus," *Philosophie und Revolution, I: Aufsätze von Herbert Marcuse* (Berlin: Philosophy and Revolution, 1967), 40–142. The essay was originally published in the journal *Die Gesellschaft* in 1932.

8

the "spectacle" started to erupt: an internationally publicized "return to Berlin" for a meeting with the Movement there, the mass of interviews, reviews, previews, and the rest. In the flurry, Marcuse's insistence that the New Left-student-youth revolt does not represent *the* revolutionary agency, but a catalyst, a "capability" of freedom, and that the present period is barely a pre-revolutionary one of "enlightenment," awakening, and struggle aimed at enlarging the scope of the subjective-instinctual break with the system—these claims, in the flurry, were obscured.

As stated earlier, the always complex, problematic, and truncated links between Marcuse's thought and the Movement are now in a state of rupture. And this particular transformation is important only as a sign and expression of larger changes in the Movement itself. There are, as it happens, far more vivid signs. At present the New Left appears to have utterly and decisively freaked out—and it may have. Normal and intense factional debate has not only suddenly been replaced by a blaring carnival of fetishized and mind-clogging rhetoric, but the rhetoric itself is "new." Actions and theories are now upheld or denounced in the name of Marxism-Leninism, proletarian internationalism, revolutionary discipline, the working class, the Black Panther Party, Chairman Mao, the National Liberation Front of Vietnam, the dictatorship of the proletariat, the seizure of state power, armed struggle, and, here and there, Stalin, Georgi Dimitrov, and the Peoples' Republic of Albania. At least momentarily, genuine *auto-critique* or critical self-reflection is scarce. For example, one faction announces that in the service of revolution there are no "adventurist" actions, and another labels the Democratic Republic of Vietnam "revisionist" and "counter-revolutionary" for participating in the Paris negotiations. Such positions are upheld by recitations of Lenin,

9

Lin Piao, and Mao Tse-Tung; in turn, they are denounced by other, apparently less crazed, factions with
other or often the same recitations from these masters.
It is as if there were a self-propelling mechanism which
brings everyone into the general reduction of *the entire
terrain* of debate and consciousness to the level of retail
sanity within wholesale madness. And there is such a
mechanism.

Since its origins in the late 1950s the New Left has
developed within a permanent and multiple crisis of self-
definition and self-consciousness. The Movement has been
precisely a movement: a process, a piercing-through the
shells of advanced capitalism and traditional socialism, a
not-yet and a to-be. It has been a project of discovering
and inventing liberatory forms of expression, experience,
organization, and struggle in a system of technically pre-
fabricated and administered life: sit-ins, building occupations, mass confrontations with authority, street fighting,
disruptions, drugs, guerrilla theater, laughter, communes.
and so forth, out of which solidarity, living human groups,
and moments of disalienation were forged and lived within
the dominant *durée* of reification, fragmentation, and powerlessness. Beneath and within this project has been the
drive toward the *coherence* of critical theory. And right
now it appears that the severity of the need for coherence
combined with the Movement's long-standing hostility to
"theory" (and theorists) as a bad trip, identical to the
asphyxiating fragments of non-thought and programmed
incoherence met in classrooms and textbooks, is finally
turning against the Movement itself. The increasingly pervasive pseudo-coherence of Marxism-Leninism, the factional bedlam, and the new cults of violence (or of workers) suggests that the continuing crisis of self-definition
and consciousness has hit a point of *implosion* and *self-*

consumption. Rapidly or gradually additional groups and individuals are pulled into the vortex. Meanwhile, a sense that the Movement is in the deepest trouble in its history is widespread; well-intended but entirely abstract appeals to unity, to an end to internecine warfare, abound. Yet as fundamental alternatives remain seemingly incoherent and fragile in comparison with the new "toughness" and the new ideologies, confusion and despair increase on the margins while the organized factions forge ahead confidently.

The shift from an eclectic and inadequate but relatively experimental and fluid "New Left-student-youth revolt" language to a progressively mechanical and self-ossifying Marxist and Leninist rhetoric is part of a new strategic intention: to transform the New Left-student revolt into (variously) a mass, anti-imperialist movement with working-class leadership; a white, revolutionary youth ally of the Black and Third World revolutionary movements; an anti-capitalist worker-student alliance. While the university campuses and high schools may, in practice, remain the Movement's central arena, the intended focus is toward factories and the streets. This shift and the increasingly brutal and systematic repression which much of the Movement as well as the Black Panthers are facing, have led to the adoption of the new rhetoric and the concepts of discipline, organization, and revolution to which it is connected. In addition, progressively apocalyptical notions of the imminence of fascism and/or revolution are both effects and contributing elements in the general hardening of lines. Thus, fairly abruptly the New Left is moving from a consciously decentralist movement with natural historical affinities to the anarchists and the anti-Leninist "workers' councils" tradition to one which begins to view the Leninist vanguard, cadre party as its organizational

11

model. The dual assumption is that in the imperialist era this is *the* model of revolutionary organization, strategy, and theory, and that the era is characterized by one "primary contradiction" (between the industrial workers and capital, or between the Third World-non-white revolutionary movements and the American empire) and thus contains "a" revolutionary class or agent (the proletariat or the anti-imperialist revolts).

Meanwhile, the infrastructure of these developments is infused with masochism, self-flagellation, and often near schizophrenia on the part of the "bourgeois" student radical. This motif has always been constitutive of the life of bourgeois intellectuals in general and radical intellectuals in particular, as well as of the New Left. Historically it has been grounded in conscious or unconscious recognition that within the division of labor in capitalist society intellectuals are parasites on the body of the working class, and this recognition is not without its genuine and progressive aspects. Yet, in the present state of affairs, where the character and function of intellectuals, students, and "mind-workers" has been drastically transformed by the development of advanced capitalism, the adoption of factory-worker, Black Panther, or streetgang ego models is absurd. It is a false and alienated overcoming of one's own alienation as a "bourgeois" student, and a suppression of the most original fact about the New Left itself: that it is not the classical breakaway intellectual vanguard whose role is to serve the impoverished against the affluent but a revolt against capitalist affluence itself, a critique of capitalist abundance as an abundance of alienation. And by denying the legitimacy of the critique of the conditions of his own existence the student radical not only recapitulates his alienation (his "untrue" existence) at a new level, but simultaneously suppresses the peculiarly explosive total critique and demands that arise out of his own alienated life.

What is happening, in its basic configurations, is hardly new; Marx himself perceived the essential element long ago:

The tradition of all the dead generations weighs like a nightmare on the brain of the living. And just when they [the radicals] seem engaged in revolutionizing themselves and things, in creating something that has never yet existed, precisely in such periods of revolutionary crisis they anxiously conjure up the spirits of the past to their service and borrow from them names, battle cries, and costumes in order to present the new scene of world history in this time-honored disguise and this borrowed language. Thus Luther donned the mask of the Apostle Paul, the Revolution of 1789 to 1814 draped itself alternately as the Roman republic and the Roman empire, and the Revolution of 1848 knew nothing better to do than to parody, now 1789, now the revolutionary tradition of 1793 to 1795. In like manner a beginner who has learnt a new language always translates it back into his mother tongue, but he has assimilated the spirit of the new language and can freely express himself in it only when he finds his way in it without recalling the old and forgets his native tongue in the use of the new.[10]

Marx goes on to emphasize, and others have pointed out, that this process of conjuring up one's progenitors in struggle can serve as a medium of deepening and illuminating one's present situation and needs. But the dominant thrust of the American New Left's sudden and enthusiastic rediscovery of Marxism and Marxism-Leninism has in actuality been regressive and repressive in precisely the terms Marx states at the same time. The fact of the mat-

[10] Karl Marx, "The Eighteenth Brumaire of Louis Bonaparte," *Marx and Engels, Selected Works I* (Moscow: Foreign Languages, 1958), 247.

ter is that in "re-Marxifying" itself, the New Left is engaged in a suppression and flight from its own most basic impulses and implications, as well as from the new scene of world history in which it stands. What has permitted the weight of the "tradition of all the dead generations" to come down on the mind of the Movement as if it were a deliverance, is that the weight of its own originality was too great to bear. The Movement's struggle to invent, create, and develop a new language, forms of organization, and a coherent critique of modern society is aborting itself in a "mother tongue" that was sclerosed and mechanical long ago; in organizational ideas that are repressive and authoritarian; and in a pseudo-coherence of abstract dogmas and myths. Concepts such as "working class" and "proletarian revolution," and "revolutionary party" become magical totems whose function is to act as mystical resolutions of real contradictions. Deflected and deformed expressions of radical and critical energy are contained in the revival of Marxism and Marxism-Leninism. The New Left is alienating itself into its own opposite.

This process of self-alienation and self-mystification is true literally, not just figuratively. The tendency, characteristic of vanguard parties and organizations of the past, to identify the vanguard with "the revolution" and "the revolutionary class" has reappeared in the Movement today. The host onto which the movement latches itself may be the working class, the Black Panther Party, or the Third World revolutionary movements: the political-psychological mechanisms involved are the same. One's own weakness and isolation, a critical apprehension of their sources, and a strategy which deals concretely with them are overcome and bypassed through a leap of faith, a linking of oneself to an apparently world-historic force. If past precedents

14

are any measure, such a leap today amounts to a bad and trite joke, if not to suicide:

Those intellectuals who fully subordinate themselves to the psychological situation of the class which in itself [appears] to represent the force of transformation and change, are led to a professional optimism and to the euphoric sensation that they are tied to an immense power. When the latter suffers severe setbacks, many of these same intellectuals face the danger of falling into a pessimism and nihilism that would be as unfounded as their optimism was. They cannot bear the fact that in particular periods it happens that the representatives of the most *avant-garde,* and futuristic thought, thought which grasps the historical situation at its roots, are necessarily isolated and forced to rely on themselves.[11]

[11] Max Horkheimer, "Traditionelle und kritische Theorie," in Alfred Schmidt, ed., *Kritische Theorie II* (Frankfurt-Main: Fischer, 1968), 163. The essay was originally published in 1937. The problems contained in the New Left's present enthusiasm for and faith in Third World revolutionary movements in particular are not only strategic in Horkheimer's sense. Rhetorical solidarity often blocks the much-needed concrete analysis of the actual relations (and antagonisms) between movements for socialism in situations of scarcity and colonialism and movements for socialism in situations of abundance and empire. Beyond this, and connected to it, the problems are also "moral." Faith, on the part of the Western New Left, in Third World "peoples' war of liberation" and in the doctrine of imperialism as a "paper tiger" is too often *both* euphorically unrealistic and immoral in the terms outlined by Rudi Dutschke: "We should be asking what difficulties of a political-strategic nature . . . are being faced by the movements in the Third World. Indeed, the forces of the Liberation Front in Vietnam are at present on the political-military offensive, but day by day the best part of the Vietnamese people is destroyed, hundreds and thousands are destroyed. To cash in on this by saying, 'the revolutionary peoples' war will win,' seems to me incorrect. Yes, Lin Piao says, 'strategically, imperialism is a paper tiger,' but tactically—and this is the situation of the Vietnamese people, the Peruvian peasants, the Bolivian fighters—tactically this situation is *miserable,* and tactically this situation is enormously difficult for us to understand." *Der Kampf des vietnamesischen Volkes und die Global-strategie des Imperialismus* (Proceedings of the International Vietnam Congress, February, 1968, West Berlin) (Berlin: Maikowski, 1968), 72.

15

Now, just when this isolation is beginning to break down, when the deep-freeze of advanced capitalism shows signs of melting, this tendency is all the more destructive because it aborts the process and struggle through which the *avant-garde* comes to itself—the only basis on which it can be of any use to anybody else.

Having begun, as the New Left has, to erect abstract bonds with world-historic forces (or supposedly world-historic forces), it is inevitable that factional lines rigidify and that one or another "deviating" faction is elevated from one that is wrong to the status of an objective agent of the ruling class. Expulsions, charges of fifth columns, "running dogs of imperialism," and the rest of the gobbledygook follow naturally. And it is not merely opposing factions that are expelled, but little bits of genuine critical theory and self-criticism accompany each deviant out of the Movement or organization. A "line" or *Weltanschauung,* that is, an "objective" body of concepts external to the concrete existence of the Movement, displaces critical thought. The dilemma, in this context, was posed sometime ago: "As long as the *avant-garde* can carry on without periodic purges, it keeps alive the hope of a classless society."[12]

The Movement's schizophrenia appears in more concrete and glaring ways. Just in the midst of the explosion of the student revolt onto a planetary scale—a fact which outside the U.S. has provoked important advances in New Left theory—the American movement is, with much fanfare, rushing to the factories to organize the workers. Significantly, the globalization of the student-youth revolt was not so much as mentioned in any published material relating to the National Convention of Students for a Democratic

---

[12] Max Horkheimer, "Autoritärer Staat," *Walter Benjamin zum Gedächtnis* (California: Institute for Social Research, Mimeo. ed., 1942), 149.

Society in the Summer of 1969. Just as commodity fetish-ism, bureaucratization, and alienation are beginning to generate disquiet, dissent, and disruption in nearly all sec-tors of American society, the New Left is putting forward a "new" critique of capitalism which describes it as a system run by a few rich men who, aided by police and military lackeys, suck the blood of the people. Such a critique is not so much inaccurate—it is not—as it is utterly fragmentary and hardly abreast of the system as a whole. Worse, it is a critique which does not contain *within itself* the germs and idea of a new society adequate to the present technological and social pre-conditions of liberation. Just at a time when the movement is beginning to experience increasingly mas-sive and systematic repression and terror—which can be met on their own terms only within the context of a decisive disintegration of the existing State and its military-counter-insurgency capability, and an equally massive, decentral-ized, and popular armed uprising; none of these conditions is present today, nor are they imaginable in the immediate future—the New Left is beginning to dabble in irrespon-sible mimicry of peasant guerrillas, gun worship, and an elevation of street fighting from a necessary tactic in many situations to the level of a strategy and even a principle of the Movement.

Within this blow-up the most regressive and disastrous element is perhaps the tendency among the Marxified and Leninized sectors of the Movement to repudiate that com-ponent of its past which linked it most closely to Marcuse. It is now claimed, for example, that the New Left has surpassed the critique of "the quality of life and culture" of capitalism, that it has gone beyond the earlier "politics of the unpolitical" to a new realism and critique of political-economy. In this respect the Movement has ironically come around to agree with those other lechers after the practical

17

and necessary—liberals and Old Marxists "sympathetic" to the New Left. For the meaning of the Movement's "politics of the unpolitical" lay in its recognition that nothing in modern society is unpolitical; that every detail of daily life is saturated with and reproduces the hegemony of the ruling system; that the object of critical thought and action is "the system" as a *totality*. In the lifetime of the New Left the commodification and bureaucratization of daily existence—that is, the transformation of life into things, functions of economic and political mechanisms—has been stretched to a breaking point and the Movement was born out of this point. One of the many implications of this fact has been that the New Left was a continual self-criticism, a refusal to recapitulate the ruling forms of life, organization, and social relations within itself. Thus, for example, it brought to the center of its activity and critique a fact previously recognized only by outcasts from the organized Left (e.g., Wilhelm Reich) and small groups of anarchists: capitalism expresses itself as much through the "authoritarian personality" it generates, as it does through the bombs it drops. (It remains to be seen whether the former is not an "organizable issue"; it is beyond debating, however, that authoritarian personalities have something to do with those who drop and want to drop bombs on peasant rebels.)

And it recognized that authoritarian and egomaniacal character structures are a deep-seated problem within the New Left itself. The choice is not between a revolutionary movement and a Left-wing "T-group," but between a libertarian and liberatory movement, and a Left-wing recapitulation of capitalist society. A dreadful legacy of traditional Marxism is the notion that the contradictions of capitalism exist entirely in the "economic base" of society, outside the individual, including the individual Marxist and the Marxist organization. And part of the original definition of the New

18

Left is its rejection of this legacy; its recognition that a coherent and unitary critique of modern society begins with a critique of individual existence. Thus the movement's "politics of the unpolitical" is not a matter of taste but a shift in the "strategy of liberation" made necessary by developments in advanced capitalism itself: it is the attempt to give life to

new needs, qualitatively different and even opposed to the prevailing aggressive and repressive needs: the emergence of a new type of man, with a vital, biological drive for liberation, and with a consciousness capable of breaking through the material as well as ideological veil of the affluent society.[13]

Apparently the Movement has outgrown such "polymorphously perverse" politics. For example, at its National Conference in the Summer of 1969, Students for a Democratic Society expelled the Progressive Labor Party—the first time in its history that SDS expelled any tendency or faction—and the ground was not that the PLP embodies a repressive, ossified, mechanistic, and puritanical ideology, but that it was objectively an agent of the capitalist state because its particular political positions on the Black Panther Party and North Vietnam were racist and counterrevolutionary. In the process the Movement's original critique of reification, authoritarianism, rote learning, hierarchy, is dropped not only in its perception of the ruling society, but in its perception and critique of itself. And these are precisely the components of the ruling society that have begun clearly to manifest themselves inside the Movement. It appears to be a law of radical politics that when the critique of the quality of life in capitalist society is dropped,

[13] Herbert Marcuse, "Liberation from the Affluent Society," *To Free a Generation: The Dialectics of Liberation* (New York: Collier, 1968), 177.

the possibility of a self-critique of the quality of the Movement is lost.

The New Left, then, is departing from the soil in which it was nurturing itself. And it is not breaking new ground but is itself being broken by the crusty and arid terrain it seems to have chosen. That few remarks "of a Marcusean or similar type" are listened to or spoken is a key symptom of these new developments, or of this return of very old developments. The Movement is "overcoming" its isolation in society (and in the universities) by metaphysical leaps into "world revolutionary" forces and into compulsive fixations on one or another single agent or revolution. That it stands in a situation which is not that of Marx, Lenin, or Mao—the nature of its own gestation and growth, the planetary explosion of student revolt, and the utopian-libertarian-experimental character of its own consciousness and activity have been partial but decisive proofs of this fact—but one in which the nature of class struggle, radical politics, and revolution assume radically *original* forms . . . all this is being suppressed by the Movement itself. Snatching up bits and pieces of rhetoric from ideological expressions of already surpassed stages of capitalist development and Left-wing movements, the New Left constructs a cocoon around its own life; it insulates itself from its own originality and desensitizes itself to the dynamic processes of social disintegration and reconstruction in motion around it.

At the time of writing, the tendencies outlined in the preceding pages are not yet closed but they are more than epiphenomenal signs. The only way of preventing their closing is for the Movement, from the bottom up, to develop its own critique of its supposedly more advanced echelons. Signs of such a reversal are present, but it is too early (and would be unjustifiably optimistic) to say that the recent degeneration and implosions are mere passing moments of regression on the road to renewal. By an odd happenstance the Movement's new period coincides with the publication of Marcuse's *An Essay on Liberation* (1969), which focuses on the New Left, among other things, and formulates thoughts of its own on possible higher stages. Marcuse, for example, argues that the present historical period and the development of the Movement in advanced industrial society necessitates a theoretical and practical move from "Marx to Fourier . . . from realism to surrealism."[14] This is a strategic and political conception, one which goes to the core of the cultural revolutionary vortex of the New Left. Its meaning may be summarized in words from the original Surrealists: "if it is realism to prune trees, it is surrealism to prune life." And here we have a perfect scenario: Marcuse, at seventy, remains true to his own and the Movement's "polymorphous perversity," while the young Movement turns on its youth in anxiety-ridden anger and embraces the maturity of tree-pruning realism. If the New Left is to renew itself, *one* of the paths it will have to travel is the one which the Movement and "ideas of a Marcusean or similar type" first met. It can and will surpass the "utopian function" of Marcuse's work only by realizing it.

[14] Herbert Marcuse, *An Essay on Liberation* (Boston: Beacon, 1969), 22.

Individuation as Praxis

Shierry M. Weber

Under total capitalist administration and introjection, the social determination of consciousness is all but complete and immediate: direct implantation of the latter into the former. Under these circumstances, radical change in consciousness is the beginning, the first step in changing social existence: emergence of the new Subject. Historically, it is again the period of enlightenment prior to material changes—a period of education, but education which turns into praxis: demonstration, confrontation, rebellion.[1]

This statement permits us to develop some important aspects of the question: what is praxis today? Traditionally, Marxism conceives a dialectical relationship between theory and praxis: theory is not disinterested but interested; it examines the present situation from the standpoint of a goal to be realized; it looks for tendencies in the present which, if realized, would lead beyond the present toward the goal. However, the goal, being something aimed at rather than something already existing, is an idea in the

[1] Herbert Marcuse, *An Essay on Liberation* (Boston: Beacon, 1969), 53.

sense in which the German idealists used the word—an ideal conception. For Marxian socialism this idea has been the nature of man. In capitalism the socio-economic order effects an alienation of man from himself; thus praxis consists in the negation of the socio-economic order through revolution, which will permit the realization of the idea of man. But it is not only that theory provides the guidelines for praxis; the historical development of the alienating socio-economic reality—of which the experience and effects of political action are a part—in turn affects theory. The goal to be realized, the idea of man, undergoes constant development, or unfolding, as reality develops; and, conversely, changes in the nature of reality can be comprehended and conceptions of the praxis appropriate to it modified only in the light of changes in the conception of the goal.

Marcuse's work represents such an unfolding of the idea of man. Traditionally, the notion of non-alienated man involved freedom, happiness, and wholeness through liberation from material oppression—that is, from the heteronomy imposed upon man when the fruit of his labor or, more fundamentally, of his actions was appropriated by others. Man's liberation from alienation was at the same time his realization as a social being (*Gattungswesen*). Marcuse extends this notion by integrating into it the realms of the aesthetic and the instinctual. This change in the idea of man is both a response to and a more adequate way of viewing the current situation. Marcuse argues that in the present social, cultural, economic system, which he calls advanced industrial society, man is exploited and alienated in all aspects of his activity and at all levels of his consciousness. His whole experience becomes false—thought becomes ideology, instinctual gratification becomes repression, needs become false needs. Thus domination extends to the instinctual level. This is why Marcuse, in analyzing subversive forces active in the present situation, speaks of a "new Subject" who would be characterized not simply by new theoretical consciousness and new understanding, but by a new instinctual orientation in which the life instincts would have ascendancy over the death instincts. The new Subject is alive, he claims, in the radical youth-student revolt, which is a revolt of the life forces against aggressiveness, ugliness, and brutality, manifestations of the death-orientation of advanced industrial society.

The revolt of the life forces is not one for beauty and sensuous gratification as opposed to freedom and rationality. Rather it is the revolt of the potentially whole man who wants whole experience. In becoming a force for liberation, the erotic instinct reveals itself to be not just the "lower" part of man but rather the energy of union and integration, in which man's higher and lower faculties are united. Hence morality, the function of the higher faculties par excellence, is actually an aspect of the fundamental erotic drive for unification:

Prior to all ethical behavior in accordance with specific social standards, prior to all ideological expression, morality is a "disposition" of the organism, perhaps rooted in the erotic drive to counter aggressiveness, to create and preserve "ever greater unities" of life.[2]

Marcuse integrates the notion of life instinct with the idea of man as the energy of wholeness; he integrates the aesthetic into it as the mode in which reason and the sensuous are harmonized (see his derivation of this conception of the aesthetic from Schiller's *Aesthetic Education of Man* in *Eros and Civilization*). In the aesthetic the senses are "self-sublimated" and reason is "desublimated." Hence in-

[2] *Ibid.*, 10.

24

terest in beauty is not simply an aspect of the current revolt; it is an awareness of the mode in which the whole man will exist in the whole society. Man as individual is whole only in solidarity with the species man; Marcuse envisages this solidarity as being realized in a non-repressive society through aesthetic activity. Given the current development of technology, life in a non-repressive society would not need to be divided between necessary and free activity; technological, practical activity could converge with aesthetic, instinctually gratifying activity:

The liberated consciousness would promote the development of a science and technology free to discover and realize the possibilities of things and men in the protection and gratification of life, playing with the potentialities of form and matter for the attainment of this goal. Technique would then tend to become art, and art would tend to form reality; the opposition between imagination and reason, higher and lower faculties, poetic and scientific thought, would be invalidated. Emergence of a new Reality Principle: under which a new sensibility and a desublimated scientific intelligence would combine in the creation of an *aesthetic ethos*.[3]

The experience of wholeness becomes part of the goal as the whole of experience becomes the object of domination. The revolt of the life instincts is the beginning of a praxis toward that goal. Praxis is focusing on and will have to continue to focus on experience. As we have seen, the dialectic of theory and praxis operates through processes. Praxis is the process through which the goal is realized. To put this in a slightly different way, the reality of the idea in us provides continuity between the present and the future in the form of a *project*, an historical possibility which we undertake to realize through action. Marcuse's notion of

[3] *Ibid.*, 24.

instinctual revolt, however, is presented not as a process or a project but as a goal, a force, and a fact. Continuing Marcuse's line of thought we come to the notion of a process of instinctual revolt, the praxis of realizing the whole man with whole experience. I shall call that process *individuation,*[4] realizing the individual. It is in this sense that in the present historical circumstances individuation is praxis.

When I say that the focus of praxis must be *personal experience* and that praxis must aim at *individuation,* this is both opposed and not opposed to what the Left commonly considers political activity. On the one hand I am saying that praxis must serve the life forces, and that focus on—for example—organizing the working class, is at present a misdirected use of energy which in effect serves the death instincts (see the section on abstract negation later in this essay). On the other hand, the commonly accepted opposition between the personal and the political only shows the extent to which personal and political experience have been rendered meaningless and ungratifying in different ways. Solidarity will be a constitutive element of the whole man; personal experience is by nature social. To imagine that the individual is a bourgeois creation or concept is to fail to see beyond the destruction of the individual in bourgeois society, where he is privatized, atomized, and put into competition with every other individual.

It is true, however, that the notions of the whole man and the individual are not immediately identical. That of the individual implies uniqueness, difference from other individuals. Nevertheless, I will argue, the whole man cannot be

---

[4] I take this term from Jung, where it refers to the process whereby the individual achieves wholeness through progressive integration of aspects of the unconscious. See, for example, "The Relations between the Ego and the Unconscious," *Two Essays on Analytical Psychology* (New York: Meridian, 1956).

whole without being individual, nor can one become fully individuated without becoming whole. Let us begin by distinguishing the particular from the individual. Consider this description of a non-individual, taken from D. H. Lawrence's *Women in Love:*

How curious it was that this was a human being: What Brangwen thought himself to be, how meaningless it was, confronted with the reality of him. Birkin could see only a strange, inexplicable almost patternless collection of passions and desires and suppressions and traditions and mechanical ideas, all cast unfused and disunited into this slender, bright-faced man of nearly fifty, who was as unresolved now as he was at twenty, and as uncreated.[5]

Lawrence's description is based on a polarity between an inexplicable, patternless collection and something united and created. He is opposing the mechanical whole, the aggregate, to the aesthetic or organic whole. A particular human being, particular in being a physical entity occupying a specific place in space and time and having a specific history, will not be exactly the same as any particular person, ·but he will not necessarily be an integrated whole. Any particular distinguishing characteristic of his will be shared by others (born in Rochester, anemic, depressed) and is thus impersonal or general—all the more so to the extent that the characteristics are socially determined. To speak in terms of the dialectic, the particular will be the general, but in an unmediated form.

In contrast, the organic whole would have the characteristics of form (pattern), meaning (explicability), and totality (unitedness). In the organic whole the general and the particular are mediated: form (itself something general) organizes the person's particular characteristics (which are

---

[5] D. H. Lawrence, *Women in Love* (New York: Ace, 1959), 202.

themselves impersonal) into a specific organization which has specific physical existence. Form means the meaningful (living) relation of the parts among each other; the resulting totality depends on the parts and vice versa. In the terminology of Kant's aesthetics, the aesthetic or organic whole is autonomous; it is purposefulness without a purpose (*zwecklose Zweckmaessigkeit*)—that is, it is not subordinated to any definite abstract concept. It is meaningful without any determinate meaning. In this sense it is living— the form cannot be separated from the actual existence; there is harmonious interpenetration of the rational and the sensuous, the general and the particular, form and matter.

This aesthetic notion of the individual as specific organic totality, however, is not completely adequate for our purposes, since it does not take into account the individual as the subject of action—as having a will—nor individuation as a process. We still do not know in what the praxis of individuation would consist. Like all praxis, however, it can occur only as the determinate negation of the existing state of affairs. Hence we must now examine in more detail the manipulation of experience, which we began by asserting it to be a characteristic of advanced industrial society, in order to conceive its determinate negation.

I have maintained that domination or oppression today acts on all aspects of experience and at the same time prevents experience from being a totality, and man from being whole. Conversely, the most important thing about the forces which destroy experience is their total—or systematic —character. It is not as though some aspects of advanced industrial society exploit labor while others manipulate consciousness. Rather, each aspect of "the system" is an element in an environment which destroys experience as such. The destructive, manipulative character of the system makes it a totality of a type different from the true whole to be realized through praxis. The false whole is perverted, ambiguous, and disintegrative. These characteristics make it difficult both to comprehend and to negate (to turn into something it is not now, by realizing alternative possibilities inherent in it).

In what sense is "the system" a false or perverted totality? The specific character of advanced industrial society derives from the conjunction of two systems or structures and the subordination of the second to the first: (1) the socio-economic structure of capitalism, which presupposes conditions of scarcity and whose characteristics include competition, private enterprise, the profit motive, class divisions, exploitation, and material inequality; and (2) modern technology as a system in which the rational, the functional, the aesthetic, and the instinctual or unconscious become fused. The notion of *rationalization* as Max Weber conceives it[6] will clarify the systematic quality of modern technology and indicate the characteristic common to capitalism and modern technology which allows them to be amalgamated in advanced industrial society.

For Weber rationalization means mathematization, efficiency, and organization; it is realized in bureaucracy. In abstract terms, it means the frictionless subordination of the particular to the abstract and formal, to the total pattern or system. The logical culmination of the process of rationalization is a system in which the distinction between form and content is obliterated because "content" itself is something formal. Thus, even better than in the creation of bureaucracy, rationalization is exemplified in the transition from "mechanical" to "electronic" technology, to use McLuhan's terms. One particularly important aspect of this

[6] See Herbert Marcuse, "Industrialization and Capitalism in the Work of Max Weber," *Negations* (Boston: Beacon, 1968).

29

transition is the development of modern design, where a system is created in which the aesthetic and the functional become identical (it thus makes art, which traditionally is not useful, obsolete). It does so by breaking down perception and motion (the bases of the aesthetic and the functional) into their most basic elements and then expressing motion in visual terms. This process allows the appearance of an object and its function to be harmonized. At the same time, modern design makes it possible to externalize and systematize the unconscious. The imagination is capable of representing unconscious instinctual materials in aesthetic form, in images, and the basic elements of visual perception discovered by modern design are thus capable of functioning as symbols of unconscious material.

An important result of the process of reduction to basic elements (which are in some sense abstract and formal) is that no particular object has value for its particularity; it is simply a combination of these basic elements. Instead, the totality, the environment as a whole, is what counts, and it becomes homogeneous, the materials of its construction being always the same. Technology creates a total environment because it is not simply abstract—the organization of a bureaucracy—but also concrete: the objects and buildings around us are part of it. The concrete is integrated into the system. This systematic, total character of modern technology has a liberating potential, as will become clear later when I discuss the notion of universalization.

Modern technology also means the development of the productive forces which produce this total environment. These productive forces are now at a level where the aesthetic ethos could function as the new reality principle, that is, a level where material scarcity is no longer necessary. However, at present technology is subordinated to capitalism and capitalist rationality:[7] that is, it is being made to serve the preservation of the present social structure, based on inequality and scarcity, and the capitalist ethos of productivity for its own sake. As a result, the systematic character of modern technology is also put to bad use. The results of this subordination are what I referred to above as perversion and disintegration.

Perverted means turned in the wrong direction, having a false objective *intention* (intention, a term from phenomenology, refers not to a psychological motive but to the fact that the significance of something is in relation to something beyond it). Capitalism perverts modern technology by turning it to false purposes, false in terms of the basic value, the notion of man discussed at the beginning of this essay. The resulting system serves not Eros, the integrating life forces, but the death instincts. In this sense it is disintegrative; it acts against integration as such, against wholeness and organic totality. It subordinates meaning, order, and form to their opposites, creating not order but a systematic and universal disorder. The perverted totality is thus neither an organic whole nor a mechanical aggregate but a homogeneous chaos.

To be more specific, advanced industrial society as the subordination of technology to capitalism serves the death instincts in the following ways: (1) it preserves need, scarcity, and inequality when these are obsolete; (2) in order to reconcile the maintenance of this inequality with the principle of productivity for its own sake, it operates through waste and destruction; (3) private enterprise, competition, and the profit motive result in anarchy in the environment (crowding, confusion, inefficiency, aesthetic disharmony) rather than in the harmoniousness and lack

[7] I cannot here go into the problem of the relation between capitalist rationality and technological rationality.

of fragmentation which is an inherent potential of modern technology; (4) in order to maintain a system in which the integrative potential of technology is frustrated, capitalism must work against Eros, through the domination of the non-capitalist world and through the manipulation of consciousness and experience to destroy comprehension and wholeness. The total character of technology is used to this disintegrative end. Modern technology as a system integrating the rational, aesthetic, functional, and instinctual can be used to incorporate all these areas of life into the disintegrative totality. The result is that the whole of life is subjected to the destruction of its own potentialities.

We must now ask what constitutes the destruction of a particular person's experience. To speak psychoanalytically (and to exaggerate), this happens when there is destruction of ego as an autonomous integrating function mediating between the unconscious and the reality principle. Instead of a confrontation of the autonomous individual with society there is *identification:*

The manifold processes of introjection seem to be ossified in almost mechanical reactions. The result is not adjustment but *mimesis:* an immediate identification of the individual with *his* society and, through it, with the society as a whole.[8]

This transformation from confrontation to identification is possible because, as Marcuse argues in "The Obsolescence of Freudian Man,"[9] the individual is no longer permitted to develop his ego within the sphere of the family before confronting society, and because the environment as a whole which, as "second nature," impresses itself upon the individual, tends to destroy integration. As a result, experience is characterized by meaninglessness, anxiety (which, as

[8] Herbert Marcuse, *One-Dimensional Man* (Boston: Beacon, 1964), 10.

[9] In *Five Lectures* (Boston: Beacon, 1970).

Herbert Fingarette argues convincingly in *The Self in Transformation*,[10] is equivalent to ego-disintegration), a sense of humiliation and exploitation, frustrated aggression, and feeling of impotence. It is not as though people are simply happy robots, secure and well-adjusted. Rather, as an essential part of the perversion, people experience their own disintegration—but in the form of increasing powerlessness (you can't fight city hall). Thus masochism has taken the place of neurosis, and cynicism and resignation are the contemporary forms of understanding.

The fact that people have feelings of anxiety and awareness of meaninglessness rather than integrated and meaningful consciousness of what is wrong indicates how the system works against the life forces. Truth, rationality, meaningfulness, and coherence are part of Eros:

Truth is a value in the strict sense inasmuch as it serves the protection and amelioration of life, as a guide in man's struggle with nature and with himself, with his own weakness and his own destructiveness. In this function, truth is indeed a matter of the sublimated life instincts, Eros, of intelligence becoming responsible and autonomous, striving to liberate life from dependence on unmastered and repressive forces.[11]

The system combats truth not by opposing it with coherent falsehood, but by destroying the very form of truth—meaningfulness and coherence. It allows truth in the service of falsehood; more precisely, it destroys meaning by making it part of meaninglessness. Hence Marcuse can speak of "the disintegration of the value of *truth*":

The media enjoy a large dispensation from the commitment to truth, and in a very special way. The point is not that the media lie ("lie" presupposes commitment to truth), they rather mingle

10 New York: Harper, 1965.
11 Herbert Marcuse, "Aggressiveness in Advanced Industrial Society," *Negations,* 266.

33

truth and half-truth with omission, factual reporting with commentary and evaluation, information with publicity and propaganda—all this made into an overwhelming whole through editorializing.[12]

The disintegration of the value of truth is an example of what Marcuse calls "one-dimensionality"—the erasing of distinctions between things that were once in opposition. Integration, the life force, works not through the abolition of distinctions but by rendering them into a meaningful, harmonious whole.

The role which the unconscious and the imagination play in disintegrated experience deserves special attention. The usurpation of the imagination and the unconscious creates two crucial forms of experience: repressive desublimation and pseudo-experience. Technological communication (particularly advertising and the media), which is part of the technological environment and shares in both its systematic character and its perversion, takes up the unconscious into the system, not only as undifferentiated instinctual energy but in the form of what Jung calls the collective unconscious—the spectrum of myth-type fantasies basic to man. There they are systematized in the form of "images." Daniel Boorstin uses this term[13] to indicate a fabricated ideal, analogue of the pseudo-event—an illusion which responds to and fosters extravagant expectations and whose artificial quality is part of its appeal. I will use the term to refer to fantasy which has the structure Boorstin describes. Within the perverted world, experience guided by images is pseudo-experience. The image is the modern, perverted form of beauty. Stendhal called beauty the *promesse de bonheur;* the image is the promise of happiness through becoming one with the technological environ-

12 *Ibid.*
13 In *The Image* (New York: Harper, 1964).

ment. It is fantasy induced, ultimately for the purpose of maintaining the status quo, to cathect the technological environment—the modly dressed happy housewife in the modern supermarket, moving rhythmically down the aisle to the sound of Muzak; the contented businessman watching a movie in the jetliner (note the interpenetration of different media, which is part of the systematic character of modern technology).

Such images are "pseudo" not because they are the products of extravagant expectations but because they are frustrating and destructive (perverted) versions of the fantasies on which they are based. Images are "object" fantasies, in which the person imagines himself as having no "subject"-ness continuous with his own experience. He imagines himself at one with the environment by virtue of becoming a sort of person by definition incomprehensible, opaque, mysterious to him—the "beautiful people," the "jet set."

The appeal of images as object-fantasies derives not only from the fact that the environment presents us with objects—commodities—which are pervaded by human significance yet have no subject-ness, but also from the fact that in the actual, perverted environment being a subject means feeling irritation, frustration, and disintegration, all of which imply unsatisfied aggression. The anarchic world around us, which seems to be bombarding us with stimuli, and the anti-meaningfulness of the media constantly provoke aggression. But this aggression remains diffuse; there is no direct personal way of expressing it. The beautiful, functional environment as a whole, the system as such, is experienced (in a confused and guilty way) as the aggressor; and any specific person, although an additional source of irritation insofar as he is a competitor, is obviously a fellow victim and therefore cannot serve as an ultimately satisfying target of hostility. Since there seems to be no way of escaping irritation, happiness, or fun, the gratification with which the environment tantalizes us can be imagined only as an escape from subject-ness.

The attempt to escape from subject-ness results in pseudo-experience—one attempts to live out an image, an object fantasy. There are ample opportunities to do so, and in doing so one experiences some instinctual gratification. The fantasy and the gratification, however, are not congruent, because one has not succeeded in escaping from subject-ness (which is by definition impossible) and because the gratification is only partial—the irritating elements of the environment always intrude into the experience. Hence there arises the feeling of not having attained the real thing, and at the same time the feeling of having been duped by the image. Thus we become gullible cynics, anxious sleepwalkers, no longer controlled from behind our backs by the unconscious but hypnotized by the externalized unconscious before our eyes. Any desire for interpersonal experience, in which we are recognized as subjects, is frustrated; people can relate to each other only through joint participation in the image. This frustration only increases the general level of hostility.

The International Situationists call this type of experience the "spectacle."[14] Direct interpersonal experience is not possible; life becomes reduced to a show in the interests of the profit motive, a display of commodities. This does not mean that experience becomes vicarious but that it becomes an act of self-consumption. Advertising makes the image a conscious fantasy, and we are consciously living it out in our daily lives. We enter the environment as consumers, and the environment of which we are part be-

[14] See Guy Debord, *La société du spectacle* (Paris: Buchet/Chastel, 1967).

comes the ultimate commodity. Since pseudo-experience is not gratifying as experience, we find our pleasure in its pseudo-ness—in the process of image-making, of techno-logical manipulation. This is why contemporary advertising no longer directly glorifies the product but rather glorifies the system—the corporate image and finally advertising itself.

Marcuse calls this sort of experience repressive desub-limation. The term indicates that limited instinctual grati-fication may be part of a totality which increases (diffuse) aggression. Sublimation, which renounces direct instinc-tual gratification for the binding of instincts in organized forms (work, aesthetic production), is more integrative than repressive desublimation. As repressive desublima-tion, the spectacle is the perversion of the aesthetic: whereas the aesthetic is a totality formed by sublimation of instincts, the spectacle releases instinctual energies but does not bind them into forms. On the other hand, the spectacle as aesthetic and as consumption prevents the individual from experiencing action and process; he is an actor only as an object and a subject only as a spectator; he consumes rather than makes. The spectacle, in the style of modern design, has no history but is only an end-less series of transformations of what is always the same. Thus the realm of the perverted aesthetic absorbs the realm of experience and action with the effect of a gen-eral disintegration and an increase in aggression.

As the determinate negation of the existing system, individuation, the process of reintegrating experience, would mean negating the most basic forms and tenden-cies of the system. In terms of of my analysis of the de-struction of experience, individuation would include the following components: refusal of the destructive forms of experience pressed upon us; recapturing the experiences of action and process; redevelopment of the ability to sublimate—to experience form, meaning, and integration; validation of subject-ness as opposed to object-ness; and de-perversion—liberation of the erotic potential of technology and men which has been distorted for the aims of advanced industrial society.

A revolt against this system and this mode of experience is in fact in process among youth, students, radicals, and hippies. Let us examine it in terms of our criteria for the praxis of individuation. It is a revolt of the life forces—against material misery, ugliness, cruelty, and in favor of happiness, peace, love, sensuality, the self, meaning, conscience. It perceives the system as a system—the capitalist system, the straight world and its way of life. And it declares itself the negation of the system. However, as the New Left turns into the Old Left and hippyism into teeny-bopperism or youth culture, it becomes apparent that the sort of negation practiced by this revolt is somehow deficient. It is, in Hegel's terminology of dialectics, abstract (indeterminate) negation. The abstract negation of x is not-x, of short hair, long hair; of being a student, dropping out. Since one-dimensional society renders oppositions non-antagonistic, abstract negation—the move to the simple opposite—is useless. Let me explain this in more detail.

(1) Abstract negation is *external*: to a gesture, an object, a style, it opposes a counter-gesture, -object, -style. But it does not negate the whole complex of forces which are concretized in the gesture, object, or style.

(2) Thus it is *ambiguous*. There are any number of different and not mutually exclusive intentions which a negative action may have.

(3) As the system works through perversion of intentions and is capable of rearranging its elements at will,

any negation can be given a perverted meaning. Thus abstract negation is *co-optable.* Hippy or radical life can itself become the content of image fantasies.

(4) Although it aims at the system, abstract negation is in fact *not total;* it is an improper response to the perception that the system as a whole is false, or an improper perception of the way in which the whole is false; for what is false is the perverted form that governs the significance of any element in the system. An aggregate of external negations does not achieve the total negation of the system.

(5) Insofar as the negation is not itself part of a project of counter-integration, it simply aids the forces of disintegration, increasing passivity, and so on. Current anti-intellectualism is an example of this.

Let me illustrate the above by polarizing the revolt into two opposing groups—the Progressive Labor Party, which to my mind illustrates the worst tendencies on the Left, and the hippies. The negative efforts of each fall within the system, which is capable of "containing" opposites conceived externally. This can be seen in the contrasting attitudes of the Progressive Labor Party and the hippies to the "self." The Progressive Labor Party rejects sex as capitalistic, long hair as narcissistic, interest in the self as bourgeois individualism. Its aim is self-denying dedication to organizing the working class (as the "opposite" of the ruling class) and to the organization that organizes the working class. This is consistent: one "organizes" objects, not subjects. The result, an authoritarian party structure and a rigidified thought-system, simply achieves through a different path what the system achieves: the negation of the potentially whole, autonomous individual.

With the hippies, the cult of the self and of sensuality also succumbs to the image mode of experience. Negative behavior and dress become a style; life becomes life-style. The external gesture is mistaken for the subjective experience. Hence the interest in astrology and macrobiotics; since the self is not experienced as subjective process, one conceives it as determined by external forces. Similarly, "doing one's thing" means choosing an activity from an approved range of "bags." Letting other people do their thing means that one takes it for granted that the other person will have only the experience appropriate to the activity he has chosen. In the case both of the Progressive Labor Party and the hippies, activity is essentially something directed by something outside oneself, and process does not enter into experience: for the Progressive Labor Party, a series of organizing gestures will magically produce the revolution; for the hippies, one bag follows another.

In each case the failure is threefold: (1) failure to understand the existing system as one of intentions, and destructive intentions, rather than institutions, behavior, or styles; (2) failure to understand the full range of what it means to be a person and thus the systematic destruction of the person; and (3) failure to understand activity, political work, the self in terms of process. Thus the current revolt, while based on some genuine refusal, is not going the path of individuation; it remains abstract negation. Determinate negation of the existing system would have to consist in using this energy of negation for a process of counter-integration, which would have the components listed above.

How can such determinate negation be possible, given that we start with a system where contradictions are not antagonistic or explosive and which operates to disinte-

40

grate rather than to integrate? In spite of this situation, the prerequisites for individuation are all present in the existing system; they derive from the nature of man as a self-conscious organism and they enter into the productive process itself. Thus they are either necessary to the system or ineradicable. These components are: the experience of time, consciousness of oneself as subject, experience of disintegration as unpleasurable, and the negative energy of refusal. As far as their integration is concerned, however, two further things must be said.

(1) Integration itself, which in the individual might manifest itself as the assumption of moral responsibility, as concentration, commitment, or creative synthesis, is both the combination of a process and an instantaneous act. As the latter it has the character of an existential decision by the subject, a decision which constitutes the subject, one which is merely internal and cannot be described, organized, or done for someone else. For instance, it is hard to speak of someone as *becoming* moral; rather, at first one sees oneself as the victim of forces outside oneself, and at some point one assumes responsibility, both for one's own participation in those forces and for the task of changing them. The assumption of responsibility is an internal reorientation, a conversion (turning around, de-perversion). On the other hand, this conversion might be the culmination of a process in which one experienced guilt for things for which he apparently was not responsible, and in which his thoughts and experiences began to focus on the problem of guilt.

(2) As I indicated earlier, the systematic, total character of modern technology has a liberating potential of its own, in addition to its potential for eliminating material scarcity. That potential consists in the creation of universality. Potentially, a technological environment is

a formal and abstract system which is universal in that the whole environment participates in it and it incorporates all aspects of experience—the rational, the functional, the aesthetic, the instinctual. Such a system is both comprehensive and comprehensible; it constitutes a range of intelligible material out of which something individual can be crystallized, articulated. Living in what Mumford calls the "neo-technic" phase of civilization, we experience this universal aspect of the technological environment as well as its disintegrative effects. This experience of the universal is decisive for the nature of possible integration today. The individual who from the beginning forms part of the "global village" (McLuhan) has available to him the universal collective unconscious of mankind. This means that the potential communication and solidarity of man is far greater than ever before; the area of potentially shared experience has been immeasurably extended. Thus the praxis of individuation must involve both universalizing the particular person and synthesizing the individual out of that universal medium. It is within this medium that the validation of subject-ness is possible— that the individual can be recognized as a specific totality and can recognize, or communicate with, others in their specificity. In the *Jenenser Realphilosophie* Hegel formulated the notion of *Geist* (mind, spirit) along these lines. In Jürgen Habermas' paraphrase:

Geist is the communication of particular persons within the medium of something general that functions as the grammar of a language does to those who speak it or a system of accepted norms to those who act and that does not give the aspect of generality primacy in opposition to particularity but rather allows the appropriate connection between them.[15]

15 Jürgen Habermas, "Arbeit und Interaktion," *Technik und Wissenschaft als Ideologie* (Frankfurt-Main: Suhrkamp, 1968), 15.

The individual who becomes integrated is capable of communicating with, that is, recognizing others. The particular person, however, experiences integration as existential decision, the expression of will. Thus if we consider political praxis as an interpersonal process, it cannot consist in organizing people as objects or persuading them to make certain gestures or perform certain actions; it must consist in helping them to work toward individuation, to enter the realm of the universal. Political praxis in this sense is analogous to the psychoanalyst's interpretation to the patient, the therapeutic intervention.[16] As Herbert Fingarette describes it:

A therapeutic interpretation given to the patient is . . . a suggestion that a new conception of one's life may be worth trying, a new 'game' played. But it is more than a suggestion about a 'conception'; it is the dynamic (existential) offering of the conception at the appropriate moment of dramatic involvement. It is more than the suggestion of a new way of talking about one's life descriptively: it is the proposal to *experience* genuinely and *see* one's life in terms of the meaning-scheme suggested by the words. It involves the hint that the structure of experience will be more unified, i.e., that there will be fewer meaningless gaps if this new scheme can become the very frame of one's being.[17]

It is as therapeutic interventions that the next sections are included. They are suggestions as to the form in which certain areas of life might be reclaimed from the existing system, that is, experienced as meaningful. They thus represent suggestions for the praxis of individuation.

[16] Psychoanalysis is a counterpart of technology as a universal system insofar as it, psychoanalysis, permits the unconscious to be assimilated into the ego as material to be integrated. Like modern design, it permits a greater fluidity between the individual and the collective unconscious.

[17] *The Self in Transformation*, 25.

I. The Exploratory Imagination—The Phenomenology of the Anti-Life

We must eat again of the tree of knowledge in order to fall back into the state of innocence.

Heinrich von Kleist, *Ueber das Marionettentheater*

What I have said about the destruction of experience is very abstract, but conclusions can be drawn from it about how one might gather data on disintegrated experience. What I shall call the phenomenology of the anti-life is a dialectical technique for doing this. Phenomenology works through concentrating not on the totality of things but on single phenomena; one "frames" a single state of consciousness while suspending one's conception of the objective structure of reality.

Dialectical phenomenology requires two slight modifications of this notion: it must focus not on single acts of consciousness but on slices of daily life, and it must be practiced on oneself. In the one-dimensional world the contrast between different spheres of life—between daily life, habit, and adventure, the out-of-the-ordinary—has been dissolved. Consequently daily life, life in the technological environment, life which is always changing but always old hat, is all there is. This is why it must be the object of our investigation. And dialectical phenomenology must be practiced on oneself, because the image mode of experience leads us to see other people as objects or antagonists, and what concerns us is the subject and his experience.

However, the phenomenological suspension of objectivity is essential to dialectical phenomenology, insofar as it involves not suspension of one's ultimate goal but of judgments as to the nature of what is going on. This suspension

44

opens one to the possibility of recognizing a greater degree of complication in reality than one's previous conception had allowed for. Equally important, it means suspension of judgments on behavior, suspension of polarized acceptance and rejections (bourgeois bad, worker good), which are the stuff of abstract negation. It means operating on the assumption that the dialectic is valid: that things may be contradictory and that one can pass through something into its opposite—that is, that one can identify with something without being reduced to it. This should indicate why phenomenology, the exploration of inner life in this society, is an antidote to abstract negation. Fear of the phenomenological suspension is fear of being overwhelmed or sucked in, of one's present identification being contradicted, of the abstract negation reverting back to its opposite, of the return of the repressed. ("I am a revolutionary, therefore I don't dare imagine what it is like to be a bourgeois because I might find out there is something nice about bourgeois life and that would show I have been wrong all this time and my whole identity would be destroyed.") This only illustrates further why abstract negation, identity that is simply the opposite of something else, is useless—it requires a paralyzing rejection of its opposite to ward off the temptation to revert to it.

Phenomenological investigation reveals that everyday experience in the perverted world takes place on various levels: (1) The pseudo-experience and its denial: One participates in certain fantasies, but at the same time does not fully admit that consciously. One both recognizes that others share the fantasy and imagines that they correspond to it without trying. (2) One discovers that acting out the fantasy is not fully satisfying, that one does not feel successfully swallowed up in the objectified image. (3) One feels used and exploited, and as a result is cranky, hostile, and

45

resentful, but also guilty. (4) Perhaps underneath all this one reaches the level of the original fantasy which makes the pseudo-experience possible and which it would be unfortunate to have to reject in trying to escape from pseudo-experience.

The value of this phenomenological undertaking consists in alienating alienation until it becomes meaningful. Consciousness becomes stretched to include other dimensions than the ones usually incorporated into theory. One experiences the totality of life in a single phenomenon, even if in disintegrated form; one sees the system reaching into individual experience and is thus forced to recognize that one shares that experience with everyone else and that solidarity is possible. And the self is stretched dialectically—to encompass contradictory feelings and different levels of experience. At the same time, the mere ability to perform the phenomenological act reveals a consciousness capable of experiencing the pseudo-world and its mechanisms; the self is thus not wholly the victim of the world. The phenomenological experience thus proves to be a source of adventure within the realm of daily life: adventure into the self through reflection on the everyday world.

II. FASHION, LOVE, SEX: RECLAIMING THE UNIVERSAL

> You could not find the boundaries of the soul, even by travelling along every path; so deep is its Logos.
>
> Heraclitus

Repressive desublimation is an example of perversion in the sense in which I have been using the term—the subordination of the particular to the general in such a way as to prevent individuation, the mediation of the particular and the general, the concrete synthesis of the individual out of the universal. Repressive desublimation, as Marcuse defines it, means both libidinal gratification in a form which subordinates libido to the death instincts and libidinal gratification in a form which promotes the subordination of the individual to a repressive social structure. I have tried to show that these two processes are equivalent in the present system.

Repressive desublimation governs the realm of sex and love today through fashion. Fashion today is a prime example of the perversion of modern design and the technological system. Whereas classical aesthetics distinguished sharply between the beautiful, in which form was the object of disinterested contemplation, and the object of desire, in which not simply the form but the material existence was crucial, in the modern technological environment the beautiful and the sexual are merged in the functional object. The fashionable woman is a human functional object; her beauty has fetishistic significance. Beauty is thus desublimated. But this desublimation is repressive—it does not permit full gratification but is ultimately frustrating. This is so first of all because fashion is fetishistic—women's clothes have the unconscious significance of disguising the fact that women are "castrated."[18] Secondly, when fashion becomes part of modern design and the women part of the total environment, fashion functions in terms of images—it is the total "look" that becomes important. It is the social system that produces the look, and beauty and sex are experienced within that form. Beauty becomes approximation to the look, sex the enjoyment of the body that has the look. The "look," however, is a general image and it is given the significance of an object-fantasy (the beautiful people);

[18] See Theodor Reik, "The Emotional Differences of the Sexes," *Of Love and Lust* (New York: Bantam, 1967), and Edmund Bergler, *Fashion and the Unconscious* (New York: Robert Brunner, 1953).

hence the experience of being beautiful and enjoying sex is not that of being oneself so much as that of approximating to the general. The more successfully one approximates the general, the more interchangeable one becomes, the more like a beautifully designed technical object. One's particular features seem arbitrary imperfections which disturb the effect. Thus the particular and the general are not mediated into individuality.

There is no need, however, to return to old-style repression, civilized morality, and modern nervousness. One can imagine an alternative to both repression and repressive desublimation. Hegel's notion of love, from the fragment "Love" published with his early theological writings, suggests such an alternative. Hegel conceives love as the process of union of the lovers, the union being the point at which each recognizes the other and recognizes himself in the other. This is possible insofar as each person becomes a subject for the other, a subject whose subject-ness is validated by the other:

True union, or love proper, exists only between living beings who are alike in power and thus in one another's eyes living beings from every point of view; in no respect is either dead for the other.[19]

Union in this sense becomes not the obliteration of individuality but its recognition: it is a union of subjects, of whole individuals. "Life senses life," Hegel says later. The notion of life is crucial here, and equivalent to Marcuse's: life is the integrating force which makes a totality of the parts:

[Love] is a feeling, yet not a single feeling. A single feeling is only a part and not the whole of life; the life present in a single

[19] Friedrich Hegel, *On Christianity: Early Theological Writings,* T. M. Knox and Richard Kroner, eds. (Chicago: University of Chicago Press, 1948), 304.

feeling dissolves its barriers and drives on till it disperses itself in the manifold of feelings with a view to finding itself in the entirety of this manifold.[20]

Whereas in image-governed love the particular is antithetical to the general, love as Hegel conceives it is the process of mediating the particular and the general. Distinctions and separateness are recognized and taken into the union. The whole person in his particularity gives himself, opens himself so as to be recognizable by the other. Love as the process of integrating such separateness has infinite content:

This wealth of life love acquires in the exchange of every thought, every variety of inner experience, for it seeks out differences and devises unifications ad infinitum . . .[21]

As part of such a project of synthesis, the commitment of two people to one another, which may be arbitrary and frustrating from the point of view of image-ridden experience, is meaningful. The stifling intimacy of most marriages or relationships of "dyadic withdrawal" arises not from excessive union but from what Hegel would call death—the discovery of dead ends, oppositions which cannot be overcome, separate elements of the lovers which are kept outside the union. Among other things, object-fantasies, which govern one's desires and cannot be satisfactorily concretized in the other precisely because the other is a specific person, might constitute such dead ends. They prevent full communication between individuals because they prevent one both from recognizing the other in his particularity and— since they represent a heteronomous power—from totalizing oneself.

Seen as part of love as the process of mediation, sex be-

[20] *Ibid.*
[21] *Ibid.*, 307.

comes precisely the opposite of what it is in repressive de-sublimation. There the body is an imperfect approximation to an impersonal technical object, and the experience of being a particular object seems to clash with it. Sartre's interpretation of sexual desire in *Being and Nothingness,* which Marcuse expounds in his review of that book, points the way to the alternative.[22] According to Sartre, the caress, which is the expression—or idiom—of sexual desire, transforms the person from a consciousness always beyond itself into body as flesh, pure existence. Thus the body is removed from the world of performance and productivity, de-instrumentalized, and made infinite in the Hegelian sense (its particular functional limitations are overcome). The experience of the body as flesh is more than the abstract negation of the body as instrument in that it permits desire to be sublimated into the realm of subjectness, of communication and recognition through the medium of the universal. The body rendered infinite becomes the medium of the language of desire, and what expresses itself in this language is the process of union, of love. The fully articulated individual dissolves into the body, into life as flesh, and the mutually understood language of sex is the expression of the mutual recognition. Thus the sexual union is both opaque, occurring in the medium of the flesh, and transparent, because of the mutuality of the idiom. As love incorporates infinite particulars into the union, the sexual idiom allows the expression of the full range of sexual fantasies and myths. As expressions of individuality incorporated into the process of communication, those fantasies need not take the form of object-fantasies, fixations; they need not constitute barrier. This is the sense in which sex can and should be polymorphous perversity.

[22] "Existentialismus," *Kultur und Gesellschaft II* (Frankfurt-Main: Suhrkamp, 1965), esp. pp. 69–75.

III. Travel and Music: Process as Adventure

> If one does not expect the unexpected one will not find it
> out, since it is not to be searched out, and difficult to
> compass.
>
> Heraclitus

Adventure means excursion into something unknown and exciting; it also means arriving somewhere. One of the characteristics of life today is that the possibility of adventure, of the out-of-the-ordinary, seems to have been foreclosed by the increasing homogeneity of the world and the increasing programming of possible experience. Travel, potentially one of the radical ways of escaping the ordinary, has become one of the most programmed of activities (see the section on tourism in Daniel Boorstin's *The Image*). What is billed as adventure is programmed impersonal fantasy, which by its very nature frustrates any desire for new experience. But the very intensity of the programming shows that travel is a potentially dangerous, that is, potentially liberating area of experience; thus the function of the programming is not, as Boorstin imagines, to make our expectations extravagant, but rather to make them limited and self-frustrating. The fulfillment of these false expectations is unfulfilling, but the transcendence of anticipations by their realization is adventure. It is certainly still possible to find the unexpected in travel, but one must know how to expect it.

One may encounter the unexpected in travel in two ways: the experience of being away and the experience of coming back. In each case the unexpected is both inside and outside oneself.

Going *away:* In life as in dreams travelling means death

51

—the arbitrary interruption of our normal life with its past-present-future continuity shaped by our projects. An American arrives in a new place, say Europe, only to find that he is *dead*—life goes on at home without him, and the new place as well is full of a life to which he is totally extraneous. Tourism is an effort at life within this death, but the life of which one is not a part is very much in evidence—hence the feeling that one did not really participate in being there. What can be learned from this death is that one is not the center of the world, something that most Americans badly need to learn.

Being away: But in fact one survives the transatlantic voyage; one lives to see the world for which one might as well be dead. One has a subjectivity which one cannot escape by being absorbed into a tourist-image. One is rather the undead than the dead. This inescapable subjectivity tends immediately to start constructing projects, plans, to relate to what is there outside. A new meaning-scheme for life may develop, incorporating the objective nature of the new place where one is. It is impossible to escape completely; as tourists frequently complain, the guided tours do not foresee all possible expenses. Thus one experiences the substitution of one meaning-scheme and life organization for another; one is forced to realize that one can survive a change of life. This experience of subjectivity depends upon an encounter with the objective nature of the other country, without which there could be no change in meaning-schemes.

Thus travel confronts us with our own project-making, meaning-scheme-constructing selves. An important aspect of this encounter is the experience of time. Travelling to a different place has the subjective effect of seeming to put us in a different time continuum. In anticipation that new time continuum takes the form of a delimited area with beginning, middle, and end. As lived, however, we experience the construction of a history—the transformation of beginning, middle, and end, into past, present, and future. It is our projects themselves that create this history by filling the time with content.

Insofar as the main project is that of assimilating the meaning framework of the other country, the experience of time resembles a rhetorical speech. Rhetoric works through varied repetition until through the listener's absorption of the material the purpose behind the material gradually becomes clear. The repeated impressions of the specific organization of the country which create a past, present, and future of understanding, comprehension, and absorption (integration) are, one discovers, equivalent.

Travel is particularly suited to teach us that experience takes place as process, because travel usually means a confrontation with history. The American's desire to see really old things and his bewilderment when he does indicate the extent to which we do not experience things as part of historical process. The American wants to experience the old, but he imagines that to do so he must experience it as new—that is, in its original state, when it had no history. In fact, the historical monument is old precisely because it has been part of a social context from its beginning until the present, when it becomes the object of tourism. Conversely, the American cannot experience the old as part of a historical continuum because he does not feel part of one himself, and thus he feels a lack of continuity between the historical and himself. The past, that is to say, cannot be experienced as present but only as past, as part of the history leading up to the present, history of which we too are part.

Travel, however, is not simply the experience of change. It involves an experimental intention, the intention of experiencing the foreign as foreign, of tentatively identifying

53

with it but never becoming completely assimilated to it. The image-beset tourist, however, wishes to become completely assimilated to the foreign without ever coming into contact with it. The different activities of the traveller and the local inhabitant insure that the traveller will be kept apart, will remain an outsider. By the same token, however, travel is always a voyage of discovery into the self as well as the external world; as part of its nature it involves that process of identification and differentiation which is part of individuation, including awareness of new experience.

The ultimate goal of the journey is the return home. The return means both the self, now discovered to be independent of any specific life-organization, confronting its former self, and the self with its new tentative meaning-scheme confronting the meaning-scheme of the homeland. One sees with new eyes to the extent that one has learned to see with the eyes of the other country. The return home confirms the self independent of the home, distanced from it by the internalized distance of the trip. Coming back brings the discovery that one can be the center of one's world.

Listening to a piece of music is in many ways analogous to a trip. Formulation of the analogy will help us both to understand the significance of travel and to see the significance of aesthetic experience in giving dimensions back to one-dimensional man. Music, like travel, involves a certain suspension of one's normal self and normal activities in the interest of expanding a more fundamental self. It delivers one over to a new time continuum (the basic rhythm of the music providing a substratum upon which a specific time structure is concretized), but one must participate in the construction within it of a new project—a new meaning-scheme based on objectively new material. In listening to a piece of music one must follow through the development of the piece itself; one is, as it were, travelling a road whose individual steps are unpredictable but meaningful, forming a totality as they proceed. The principle of variation in classical music (the musical equivalent of rhetoric) in which a stable identity is the basis of novelty, difference, and the unexpected, illustrates this process: the unfolding of the potential inherent in the original theme, the repetitions which constitute the history of the theme, and finally the recapitulation, which reveals the meaning of the whole now embodied in the original. The perversion of the aesthetic experience of music into repressive desublimation is present in rock music, one primary intention of which is not totalization but disintegration: the basic rhythm becomes an end in itself, and repetition and noise act to break down the ego to permit the diffuse release of sexual and aggressive energy, thus substituting annihilation and explosion—escape from the self—for discovery and integration.

IV. Vegetarianism: The Experience of Praxis

> It is natural that big fish eat little fish—though it may not seem natural to the little fish.
> Herbert Marcuse, *One-Dimensional Man*

Let us examine seriously what would be involved in an individual's decision to become a vegetarian—to refrain from eating meat (including fish, seafood) because animals must be killed to produce meat. What is the value of such a decision? Animals are still being killed to produce meat, other people are still meat-eaters, and the individual is deprived of the pleasures of a certain number of meat dishes and has incurred the trouble of finding non-meat things to eat. Not a political but a purely individual act, masochistic and moralistic, one tends to say, and there are many more important things to be done.

Now let us look at the decision "ideally," so to speak. It is obvious that it is immoral to kill animals for food. Suffering is bad, even if in some cases it might be an inevitable by-product of attaining some goal. Animals suffer; and in raising and killing them for our ends we are making them objects, denying them control over their existence. As is always the case in master-slave relations, the masters, those who kill for food, do not escape the consequences. The criminal's punishment is his crime, said Hegel. By separating ourselves from nature, in decreeing ourselves its judge, its masters, we place ourselves in conflict with it and make aggression and destruction part of our fundamental experience of the world. To someone in our culture it seems obvious that a cannibal's experience of people would be fundamentally deformed by his cannibalism. Similarly, our experience of life as natural phenomenon is changed by our practice of killing animals.

Furthermore, disregarding the question whether it was ever *necessary* to eat meat, it is certainly not so now. The human race possesses the means to nourish itself without killing animals. In Marcuse's terms, killing animals today is "surplus repression," destructive both for the animals and for ourselves. If, then, one wished to realize the current possibilities for a non-repressive civilization, they would include vegetarianism. The goal of the whole man outlined at the beginning of this essay involves a non-destructive, harmonious relationship to internal and external nature. This does not mean a return to the non-rational state of nature but rather what Marcuse calls the "pacification" of nature. Man must not only cease to dominate nature but he must help it to self-sublimation: "Civilization produces the means for freeing Nature from its own brutality, its own insufficiency, its own blindness, by virtue of the cognitive and transforming power of Reason."[23] Man's harmonious integration with his environment means a harmonious integration of reason and nature in nature itself. The fact that some animals are not vegetarians, that is to say, does not mean that man has the right to imitate them.

If we confront this ideal of vegetarianism with the present reality, what do we find? A society in which the production apparatus includes a meat-producing industry. Originally we ate meat simply because it was one available form of nourishment; getting that nourishment was part of the process of mastery of nature. Now we eat meat because it is part of the organized process of life in our culture. Unconsciously we connect it with aggressive-sadistic fantasies, but because we do not participate immediately in the killing process, we feel no responsibility for it, nor do we get direct satisfaction of aggressive drives. We are simply cogs in the wheel, like Eichmann.

Why, however, would not radicals committed to a different form of society and recognizing eating meat as cruelty, not simply refuse to participate, become vegetarians? Obviously, some have, but most do not take the question seriously. I suggest that this simply indicates the extent to which we participate in repressive desublimation, the liberation of a restricted area of instinctual gratification in forms which have the result of increasing society's control over the individual and strengthening aggression while weakening the life forces. Repressive desublimation brings physical pleasure—comfort, good food, sex, and so on. One's general experience of the world, however, is of a place unpleasurable, chaotic, hostile, and frustrating. Thus one is unwilling to imagine that pleasure can be part of oppression; are we

[23] *One-Dimensional Man,* 238.

not revolting for more pleasure? Furthermore, merely physical experiences have been so highly elaborated and serious thought so disintegrated that it seems inconceivable that something involving the body—food—could have moral significance. One might rebel against being poisoned by preservatives or polluted by industry, but the thought of renouncing physical pleasure on moral grounds simply does not arise. For all these reasons, radical action based on justifiable hostility, opposition, and violence is more appealing than action like vegetarianism, which not only does not involve violence but also means renunciation of pleasure. All this, however, only reveals our fragmentation and the extent to which even radical political praxis is governed by socially manipulated instinctual processes rather than by an integrative moral faculty.

The value of becoming a vegetarian should now be clear. Vegetarianism, like the praxis of individuation in general, entails making one's own experience and actions continuous with the goal to be realized. It constitutes praxis not as immediate action upon society but as part of the creation of the new subject. That is to say, it is of no significant help to animals, who are still slaughtered, nor does it act against the food industry, though that might become the focus of collective action. It does, however, effect a change in the individual. It allows him to recognize that there can be moral action, that it is possible to break with the false totality, the production-apparatus' organization of daily life. In acting, he assumes the individual responsibility which is his but which is hidden by the feeling of being a helpless victim. As in all praxis, he changes from being a passive accomplice in social crime to a free individual who is part of a potential group of free individuals. That is, by renouncing the role of dominator of nature, he experiences the difference between making something into an object and recognizing it as a subject; he thus rejoins the community of beings. But the most specific value of vegetarianism is as action against false needs and repressive desublimation. The vegetarian de-represses an area of daily life—he can experience the destructiveness involved in killing animals because he no longer needs to hide it from himself, and he can experience the falseness of needs and pleasures because he is capable of renouncing them.

Until now I have talked primarily about inner experience, psychic change. What I have just said should indicate that action or behavior is an essential part of experience. There are certain experiences one can have only by acting, and certain experiences which are realized in decision and consequent action. One can recognize that one is treating something as an object and decide to treat it as a subject, but one cannot "theoretically" recognize it as a subject and continue to treat it as an object. If it is true that individuation is praxis, it is equally true that praxis is individuation.

Reversals and Lost Meanings

RUSSELL JACOBY

Marcuse's essays: "Socialist Humanism?" "The Obsolescence of Marxism?" The question mark, as Marcuse himself has written, is the dialectic crystallized. The period periodizes thought, slices it, and ends it. Period. The story has been told. Everyone go home now. It hands thought over manhandled to those who would with pleasure contemplate the end, if it furnished more story. The question marks the story still to be made, and still to be told; story passes into history, the history of the here and now. The question is a sounding of the human factors and human actors that will make it so—or not; its hesitation is that of man himself. The period silences the sounds in its rush to reify. The rush itself betrays nervousness. The story is told all too fast as if it were the doctored version it is.

The story is in on Marcuse also. Commentary already abounds; the questions answered, the conclusions drawn. That his own works have so quickly become victims of the forces they exposed, testifies to the truth of his analysis— and to the strength of the forces. The "culture industry," with an unerring instinct for growth potential, cashes in on

60

radical thought, stock-piling critical theory for private use, as if to stun possible practitioners into inactivity by the accumulated reserve. Here, as elsewhere, domination grows fat and sleek on its own exposé, on its own story. Marcuse, in a small essay, "Zur Stellung des Denkens heute," reformulated his citation of Ernst Bloch in *One-Dimensional Man:* "Ernst Bloch's words: 'That which is cannot be true' are from 1918. Since then the world has altered; the existing order speaks the truth about itself, publicizes its truths and its deeds."

Domination goes public and does well. As the effects wear off, the dose is doubled; no one can get enough of the same. The statement of the Situationists is to the point: "The revolt is contained by over-exposure; we are given it to contemplate so that we shall forget to participate." The erudite and not-so-erudite commentaries, recapitulations, and summaries of Marcuse serve to contain that which their subject is out to explode.[1] To locate Marcuse in the German Hegelian renaissance spurred by Lukács, or to classify him as a rebelling but faithful student of Heidegger is to do one's bit to people the nightmare of history; the classification of intellectual origins assures the might of the past by snuffing out the new; in deriving the critique it avoids confronting it. Hegel's pessimism or Reich's left Freudianism is chalked up as the winner. To explain, wrote T. W. Adorno, is to explain away.

The period adds its 2¢ to the accumulated common sense: there is nothing new under the sun. The question mark is a fragment of the hope that has yet to be justified: is there anything new under the sun? Socialist humanism is not a reality, nor a necessity, but a possibility. The question mark in "A Biological Base for Socialism?", a chapter in *An*

---

[1] One work of this genre merits special distinction: J. M. Palmier's simulation of research and thought in his *Sur Marcuse* (Paris: "10–18," 1968).

Essay on Liberation, is both an appraisal of the possibilities and a call for praxis; to make socialism biological. Marcuse's formulation in *One-Dimensional Man* of the Marxist dialectic of freedom and necessity in history is the "realm of chance in the realm of necessity." The question mark is a reading of the chances in question to the point that human actions determine, and are not determined; it tells what can or may be, evoking the classic formulation: socialism or barbarism?

The effort to recapture lost meaning, to recall the repressed concreteness, traverses all of Marcuse's work from his early essays through *An Essay on Liberation.* The task of dialectical thought, Marcuse wrote in *Reason and Revolution,* is inseparable from the recovery of meaning, the return or rather the conscious liberation of the repressed. The words that bespeak terror and unhappiness but speak only of satisfaction and approval must tell what they hide. Mutilated not beyond, but to a recognition that mirrors a familiarity that never existed, language deals a deadly blow to critical thought.

"The rupture with the continuum of domination must also be a rupture with the vocabulary of domination," Marcuse tells us in *Essay on Liberation.* The metaphysical "ghosts" that contemporary analytic philosophy is out to purge from the language are but the frightened remains of a language haunted with real terror; the ghosts must be made to haunt the language again. The secular language which from Huss to Luther was once the language of resistance, must fulfill its original task and become a *Volkssprache* against those who oppress the people.

But now the people's language is the language of domination. And to the point that the language is homogenous and uniform it corrupts the resistance that uses it; the attack itself sustains and strengthens that which is attacked. Indistinguishable from its object, the critique is swallowed; the language bemoaned as bankrupt is granted just enough life to preserve its reign.

And yet the impulse that in part was Dada's seems already past. Jacques Vaché, who inspired André Breton, wrote next to nothing. Refusal refused to sustain the object, which though unconcerned sustained itself. Hence the only choice: to build on the remnants that after the sack were left behind. Language must be made to accuse itself while surpassing itself, to speak its own and another language. To Marcuse slang is a beginning, telling it like it is with the words that do not. So too do the graffiti and the "Marxist cartoons" of the Situationists accuse as they express; the playboy model announcing that the ruling class is frigid threatens the monopoly of sex and pleasure in the very symbols that are to affirm it.

What is in question is the place of traditional treatises and analyses. The language bought out wholesale by the big interests, muting truth by depriving words themselves of meaning, leaves traditional critical thought wordless. The remaining fragments form obscure patterns—a mark of truth in a world where clarity is a lie. Hence Max Horkheimer, in the dark hours of World War II, called for a language not easily understood: to be understood is to be misunderstood; to be read is to be misread. And insofar as Marcuse's works are couched in the language and style of ordinary discourse; and insofar as he tries in interviews and essays to be more and more accessible, his works too are victimized, and left depleted to speak the truth in the language of lies.

The young *contra* the old—a conflict as old as the old and the young, the fathers and the sons. These young— students, militants, and others—have moved to the center of Marcuse's political analysis of the internal resistance to advanced capitalism, earning the dedication of *An Essay on Liberation,* and praised in nearly all his recent writings. Their opposition marks a "turning point," forming, to be sure, not the revolutionary subject itself, but that of a "preparation," of a "stimulus." Their opposition, anchored in their bodies, instincts, and metabolism, exactly where they are threatened, in turn threatens the apparatus precisely at its source of aggression and violence. "Make Love, Not War" is more than a slogan, Marcuse writes in a "Political Preface 1966" to *Eros and Civilization;* the instincts of life and love are not reconcilable with the reality of a murdering and murderous establishment. "The fight for eros is a *political* fight."

And yet youth is less than a rebel, as Marcuse himself has analyzed—and forgotten? Sold out before they can sell out, they bow first and without reserve before advanced domination, completely forgetting what they never knew, that there is an alternative. The formation of the ego as drawn by Freud belongs already to surpassed historical conditions, Marcuse tells us in an essay, "The Obsolescence of Psychoanalysis," and *Eros and Civilization.* The family and the father are remnants of obsolete power, dated by the more concentrated and efficient forces that bypass these mediations to directly command the unresisting child. Fatal for critical thought is that the scars left from the individual confrontation of child against father, family, and state, which produced the ego and sustained ultimately autonomous consciousness itself, pass to a scarless ego/superego that knew no battles and speaks only in the name of the unchallenged victor. "In the struggle between generations," Marcuse wrote, "the sides seem to have shifted; the son knows better; he represents the mature reality principle against its obsolete forms." Liberation is shelved; the dispute is only over the pickings: who gets the car?

The latest in domination is parodied as the final liberation by youth fabricated in the image of the market. The surplus products find their ultimate consumer willing to discard as dictated. "Planned obsolescence," the invention of an unplanned and obsolete economy, exposes its full unreason, applying indifferently to things and men; the products fixed to break, mirror a youth programmed to be junked. The fetish of youth helps keep the show on the road.

The young left is not immune. The instinctual revolt that to Marcuse is a hope is crystalized in the phrase "radical life style," that style of life that rejects the clothes, the sex, the commodities of the bourgeois life. Yet the words themselves are revealing. The "style" threatens to become what it is—a style, to be picked up or dropped, marketed or phased out, adorning lives radically the same. The giant photographs of "Ché" and Mao replace the writings, and titillate without stirring the revolutionary aspirations. The radical clothes replace the deed. Fashion, charged with the mission of renovating the monotonous, cashes in. "Fashion," wrote Walter Benjamin, "prescribes the ritual which determines how the fetish will be honored . . . Fetishism which succumbs to the sex appeal of the inorganic is its vital nerve."

And yet youth rebels, in words, in deeds, in numbers, refuting not Marcuse, but his interpreters. To read Marcuse one-dimensionally is to be revictimized. The contradictions exist and are expressed, however manipulated. Youth is one of them. The youth rebellion is manufactured, but it is also real. Here as elsewhere the hint and praxis of liberation mixes with its denial which would alternatively sell or crush it.

Youth remains more than the object it is made to be; that fashion closes in indicates the subject is getting restless. The statement of the Situationists is as true as Benjamin's. "Fashion accelerates because revolution is treading on its tail." Even if the refusal itself is fetishized and affirms, it harbors the threat of the rejection of the fetish. The negative in the advanced industrial countries exists in the only manner it can, sullied to the core. The refusal short of political praxis in the streets and which cannot be commoditized is unknown—for the very reasons that make it necessary. The impulse that is youth's does not of course escape; but to take the fetish and fetishize it again is, to follow T. W. Adorno, to capitulate to the appearance, dismissing so as to render impotent the power of the negative. Rather, the task is to strengthen, not enfeeble, the negative, no matter its polluted condition; it is to undo, not second the fetish. The reading of the conflict as only that between under- and over-25-year-olds, and counseling and predicting its disappearance with age, is also an age-old stand, endorsing the strength and endurance of the given. Youth is more than lacking in years; rather its fidelity to the instincts of life defines the young. In this some of the young are old, and some of the old are young. And that is the hope, that youth will preserve itself transcending the years, not in accoutrements and commodities, but in the need and desire to be free. Marcuse is a case in point; to figure his age only in years is to trample with positivism a life's work of dialectics.

The dog is man's best friend; but this is a dog's life, fit only for a dog. The dog is to be esteemed and pampered in exchange for a loyalty that man cannot provide; but it is also to be whipped and beaten back to the life of the wolf from which it came. The contradiction exists as much or as little with women, in its "classic" form situated in the 19th century: some domesticated, restricted to the home, idealized and honored, and others victimized by the market, sought as the cheapest factory labor, brutalized and manhandled. Displayed is the diffusion of instincts outlined by Freud. Oversublimated eros toward some women is revenged by raw aggression toward others. Women beyond and outside love exist by virtue of others beneath love. That which is domesticated—woman or dog—is sustained by that which is wild, that which is *made* wild.

The domesticator is haunted by the bestial; his roots and desires are in the wilds. In the name of civilization he incessantly violates man and nature, leveling that which suggests his reign is not total, and hence vulnerable; he violates to keep the distance, fearing the return he nearly wants. Consciousness of his secret affinity to the bestial surfaces only at night in the eerie tales and nightmares of she-wolves, and wolf-men, and blood-sucking man-animals. The horror of the savagery of these tales of men-turned-beasts feeds off the reality, and Freud has taught us that the eerie and uncanny is anchored in the familiar and the intimate. The strange is a return of the familiar. The strange tales of violence and blood, revealing man's relation to nature, are part of the not-so-strange continuum of man's malpractices. The psychoanalyst corrects the humanist: nothing bestial is alien to me. The history of the nightmare is a clue to the nightmare of history.

To N. O. Brown the tale of the wolf tells the whole story. The archetypal city, Rome, was founded by Romulus and Remus, the sons of the she-wolf; their festival was that of the wolf "at which youth naked except for girdles made from the skin of victims ran wild through the city, striking those whom they met, especially women, with strips of goat skin," and their politics was that of crime. The fratricide of

Romulus set the unchangeable pattern for all succeeding republics: "All fraternity is fratricidal."

Marcuse's formulations are different, belonging to that social theory that has not glorified the natural at the expense of the human, nor the human at the expense of the natural. The dehistoricization of history by way of nature, the favorite method of justifying the evil and unjust as timeless and unchangeable, is rejected as is the dehistoricization of Nature, that leaves it as stuff to be beaten and brutalized endlessly. Marcuse, like Marx: neither confuses the human with the natural, nor renders them utterly distinct.

To follow Marcuse, the necessity of subjugating Nature entailed the subjugation of man himself: this historical "project" deformed from the beginning the subject/object, man/nature relation. The "subject that has conquered matter," wrote Marcuse in *Reason and Revolution,* "suffers under the dead weight of his conquest." Violence against nature is sustained by violence against man. "The ego," Marcuse tells us in *Eros and Civilization,* "which undertook the rational transformation of the human and natural environment revealed itself as an essentially aggressive, offensive subject, whose thoughts and actions were designed for mastering objects. It was a subject *against* an object." And "Nature (its own as well as the external world) were 'given' to the ego as something that had to be fought, conquered, and even violated . . ." This internal conquest of man himself "culminates in the conquest of external nature, which must be perpetually attacked, curbed, and exploited in order to yield to human needs . . . Nature is *a priori* experienced by an organism bent to domination . . ."

If, as Spengler has written, imperialism is civilization unadulterated, Nature was the first colony. Here the relation of violence and suffering, domination and liberation is played out in its most original and mute form. The chain of violence begins here with the domesticator who, in taming, releases raw aggression. Only the acute, like Rosa Luxemburg, have picked up this repressed and essential link in the continuum of domination. Her sentiments from inside prison have their reason:

. . . The buffaloes are war booty from Rumania . . . They have been accustomed to the luxuriant Rumanian pastures and have to put up with lean and scanty fodder. Unsparingly exploited, yoked to heavy loads, they are soon worked to death. The other day a lorry came laden with sacks, so overladen indeed that the buffaloes were unable to drag it across the threshold of the gate. The soldier-driver, a brute of a fellow, belabored the poor beasts so savagely with the butt end of his whip that the wardress at the gate, indignant at the sight, asked him if he had no compassion for animals. 'No more than anyone has compassion for us men,' he answered. . . . The one that was bleeding had an expression on its black face and in its soft black eyes like that of a weeping child. . . . Far distant, lost for ever, were the green lush meadows of Rumania. How different, there the song of the birds and the melodious call of the herdsman. Instead the hideous street, the fetid stable, the rank hay mingled with mouldy straw, the strange and terrible men . . . Poor wretch, I am as powerless, as dumb as yourself; I am at one with you in my pain, my weakness, and my longing . . . [Meanwhile] the driver, hands in pockets, was striding up and down the courtyard, smiling to himself as he whistled a pop air. I had a vision of all the splendor of the war.

The liberation of man is the liberation of nature and man, the liberation of the dog/wolf and the life fit for a dog; it is the resolution of the tamed and the tamer, the violated and the violator. Yet nature liberated is not nature freed from man; nature suffers on its own as well as it is made to suffer. "Suffering, violence, and destruction," Marcuse writes in *One-Dimensional Man,* "are categories of the natural as well as human reality." The natural, as nature untouched, is brutal and unnatural; it is natural "that big fish eat little fish—though it may not seem natural to the little fish." If, as Marx has said, man becomes human when his human nature becomes for him natural, so too does nature become natural when its nature becomes its own, when it is humanized. Marx elsewhere quotes Thomas Münzer. "It is in this sense that Thomas Münzer declares insupportable 'that all the creatures be transformed into property, the fish in the water, the birds in the air, the plants on the ground: the creatures must also become free.' "

Not pessimism, but optimism and resignation, bow before the given. Both of the latter, secretly or openly, posit an inhuman mechanism as the essence of reality, only reading it differently. The inorganic is to move, or not to move, of its own accord. The wait-and-see attitude of the hopeful or hopeless spectator is strongly recommended, and to those who have waited and seen, strongly enforced. Reification is promoted or decreed as the most effective way of ending reification; the subject is picked off the scene and told to read all about it. Even the opposition takes up, on occasion, the same form of official optimism, preserving the static by endlessly predicting change to the impatient. The supreme optimism and confidence of Kautsky's ilk, which assumes that victory is automatically assured, proscribes human action as neatly as the establishment that needs none. Optimism is the grease, and resignation the soup, for the drudgery of everyday life.

Pessimism is optimism without illusion; it holds out the hope for change, not its necessity, with a sensitivity to the might of its denial. For Marcuse pessimism is a function of the importance that is bestowed on the human subject as

70

actor. Reality on its own guarantees nothing but more of the same; to be won it must be acted upon and refashioned. Marcuse follows the Lukács of *Geschichte und Klassenbewusstsein:* "The blind power of the motor-forces does not lead 'automatically' to their goal," the inevitability of the transition to socialism is only as inevitable as men by a free act make it so. The stuff of reality itself, if not restructured by conscious human subjects, assures the continuance of domination even after a collapse. Progress in human liberation necessitates the reversal and redoing of what has passed for progress. Marx himself, Marcuse writes in *Das Ende der Utopie,* too wedded to the "concept of the continuum of progress," underestimated the break, change, and distance that separated the old from the new. The human subject is the reality that makes or breaks, forms or deforms, the revolution.

Pessimism plumbs the depths, sounds out the power and hold of the existent, and finding more than a power clique blocking the free society, does not give up the struggle but deepens it. *Eros and Civilization* by Marcuse's own admission is an optimistic book, sketching the possibilities of a liberated society; but it is also his most pessimistic book, not in tone, but in the analysis of the "dialectic of civilization" that has condemned all progress, all revolutions to betray their promise. Counter-revolution is defined by more than external might. Marcuse follows the earlier Reich: it is biologically anchored in the revolutionaries themselves. The instincts, victims of the past, are not to be put off by tactical considerations or political victories in their drive to re-establish the slain fathers, to re-install domination. The combined weight of centuries of domination more than rigs the chances, but the response is not resignation—nor optimism—but rather the attempt to end the horror show on the level at which it is continually replenished, the instinctual.

71

The submerged inner connection between pessimism and optimism emerges. Marcuse's formulations of possible forms of eros in *Eros and Civilization* are as optimistic as his analysis is pessimistic. The same *Eros and Civilization* contains a defense of Freud's pessimism against the confidence and the good cheer of the neo-Freudians. It is the former which, in its refusal to underestimate the toll and depth of the existent repression, suggests possibilities for liberation smothered by predictions and instructions for happy love and secure lives. The refusal contained by pessimism preserves the utopia buried by the optimism that confounds the given with its negative.

The pessimism is an appraisal of the chance. The might and violence of the denial have been, and are, only too apparent. "The events of the last years refute all optimism," wrote Marcuse in a preface to *Eros and Civilization:* Or equally, the events of the last centuries refute all optimism. To these events, to these years, pessimism remains faithful; it is saturated with history, the history of suffering and want. Memory is the ground of pessimism, memory of the species and the individual: human history. To Marcuse memory is the congealed history of forgotten hopes and brutal denials. To forget that which was is to collaborate with the new that pretends to be different. "To forget is also to forgive what should not be forgiven . . . Such forgiveness reproduces the conditions which reproduce injustice and enslavement; to forget past suffering is to forgive the forces that caused it— without defeating these forces. The wounds that heal in time are also the wounds that contain the poison." To remember is part of the challenge, the refusal; it is to exchange for the optimism that would in good consciousness forget and repeat the bad, the pessimism that recalls and examines the repressed past so as to annul it.

Pessimism is a ruthless appraisal of a ruthless world; it

72

insists on uncompromising clarity. "A certain form of pessimism carries with it a lucidity," wrote A. Artaud, ". . . the lucidity of despair." Action is not curtailed, as with resignation or official optimism, but is projected and deepened by the theory that shuns only dogmatism. Marcuse in a "Nachwort" to an edition of the *Eighteenth Brumaire* cites Marx's words of 1850 condemning the idealistic and dogmatic analysis by some comrades for the immediate possibilities for revolution and adds: "The consciousness of defeat, even desperation, belongs to the truth of the theory and its hope."

The Critical Theory of Society:
Present Situation and Future Tasks

WILLIAM LEISS

During the nineteen-thirties authors associated with Frankfurt's Institute for Social Research developed a framework
for the analysis of contemporary society and its historical
roots which they called "the critical theory of society."
Among them it was Max Horkheimer, the first director of
the Institute, and Herbert Marcuse who gave the most explicit accounts of the scope and intentions of this critical
theory.[1] Since that time the work of the three best-known
representatives of the Frankfurt Institute (Horkheimer,
Marcuse, and Theodor Adorno) has become widely recognized in Europe; in the United States, however, Horkheimer's name is virtually unknown in the academic
environment and Adorno is known almost exclusively in
connection with *The Authoritarian Personality*. Of course
Marcuse's recent public notoriety has called attention to

[1] Max Horkheimer, "Traditionelle und kritische Theorie," in Alfred
Schmidt, ed., *Kritische Theorie II* (Frankfurt-Main: Fischer, 1968),
137–200. Hereafter this collection of essays is referred to as *KT*. Marcuse, "Philosophie und kritische Theorie," in English translation
"Philosophy and Critical Theory," *Negations: Essays in Critical Theory*
(Boston: Beacon, 1968), 134–158. These essays were originally published in the *Zeitschrift für Sozialforschung* in 1937.

his books and articles in the United States well outside of "New Left" circles, and the first signs of a wider official acknowledgment of his writings on the part of "serious" scholars in this country are appearing.

In Europe at present the activities of the Frankfurt Institute continue under Adorno's inspiration, and younger persons associated with it, especially Alfred Schmidt, have already produced an impressive number of articles and books. A full-scale study of critical theory has been published there recently.[2] But in this country the Institute's contribution—and indeed the contribution of the twentieth-century European Left in general—to radical social thought and action has been barely recognized, much less critically evaluated and applied, either by academic specialists or by non-academic radicals. A few doctoral dissertations along these lines are in progress or have been completed recently, and some of this material will undoubtedly be published in the coming years. But a concerted effort will be required in order to repair the damage done to both social science and radical politics by this lengthy neglect of the extensive effort undertaken in Europe throughout this century to revitalize the intellectual foundations of the modern revolutionary tradition.

Full studies of these materials and translations of the important sources are essential, then, for radical action in this country. In the meantime the general issue concerning the problems and purposes of the contemporary study of society—specifically, the study which attempts to contribute to the radical change necessary to bring about a truly human social order—must be always in the forefront of our work. In the present essay I propose to discuss that issue

[2] Gian Enrico Rusconi, *La teoria critica della società* (Bologna: il Mulino, 1968).

in relation to the very broad outlines of the critical theory of society. The specific purpose of this essay is to ask what is the present situation of the critical theory and what are its future tasks.

It is not only the needs of social science and radical politics, but also the internal development of critical theory itself, which necessitates this current evaluation of its situation and possibilities. In the opinion of those who developed the theory, changing historical circumstances from the nineteen-thirties to the present require important modifications in its basic approach to social problems. We shall discuss this problem below. In addition, the practical response of the theory's founders to some recent political issues has clearly shown that serious differences exist among them in terms of what guidelines for contemporary political action might be drawn from the theory. Whereas Marcuse undertook a strenuous public campaign against the war in Vietnam, Horkheimer has been sympathetic to the position of the United States and critical of the youthful West German antiwar protesters. Secondly, Marcuse and Adorno have responded quite differently to certain issues concerning the student movement within the universities. As a result of both theoretical and practical difficulties, the future of critical theory is in doubt.

I

The critical theory of society is the ongoing analysis of modern society which has as its basis the work of Marx. As it is used in this phrase, the term "critical" refers specifically to the critique of political economy which constitutes the core of Marx's efforts.[3] Yet the situation is not so simple,

[3] *KT II*, 155 fn., 192; *Negations*, 282, fn. 18.

for there is a great deal at stake in the matter of the way in which Marx's work is understood and applied. The contemporary critical theory of society attempts a creative recovery and development of its nineteenth-century inheritance, and its cardinal principles are: (1) the concrete social reality is always changing, even though the basic social form (such as bourgeois society) persists; (2) theoretical constructions are a part of that concrete social reality, and thus their modification is a response to an objective necessity. In Horkheimer's words (*KT I,* 49): "The theoretical activity of men, just like their practical activity, is not the independent recognition of a stable object, but a product of the changing reality." This theory implicitly reinforces the crucial point that dogmatism and uncreativity in the understanding of Marxism injures not the representatives of the established order, but rather the forces struggling for a better society.

The essential difference between the critical theory and the other predominant contemporary modes of theoretical analysis, however, is not that it defines itself as "Marxist" vis-à-vis "non-Marxist" attitudes. Since the theoretical and practical heritage of Marxism is itself an integral part of the ongoing historical dynamic, Marxism cannot hope to stand outside this dynamic as a completed and self-sufficient entity. Since its fate is bound up with the general fate of the bitter struggle for a rational human society, and since the outcome of that struggle will remain in the balance for a long time yet, Marxism necessarily undergoes modifications insofar as the specific content of its basic concepts is concerned. This is not by any means an opportunistic adaptation to current reality undertaken to "save" the theory, an ideological venture by the faithful, precisely because this theory played a profound role in the *creation* of the current historical reality: The changing reality within which it oper-

77

ates is itself partially a product of the theory, and in a sense the changing theory is responding to the conditions of its own success as a determinant of historical development.

What is then the essential difference between critical theory and the other major types, which Horkheimer groups under the name of "traditional" theory? For traditional theory, and all of the investigations of the modern social sciences that have been undertaken in accordance with its presuppositions, the actual social context of the theory and the ends served by it remain external—that is, formally extrinsic—to the theory itself. In fact this theory strives constantly to free itself from all "prejudices" and "interests," and in one of its late forms claims "value-free inquiry" for its rubric. The critical theory, on the other hand, incorporates a determinate goal in the structure of its analysis and explicitly sees itself as "an inseparable moment of the historical effort to create a world adequate for the needs and powers of men." Horkheimer maintains that

. . . in the constitution of its categories and in all phases of its progress critical theory is guided by the interest in the rational organization of human activity, which also is concerned with clarifying and legitimizing the theory itself. For it is not only a matter of ends that have been already indicated in the present forms of life, but of men with all their possibilities.[4]

Is this commitment of the theory to the achievement of a rational form of human society merely an arbitrary act? Or worse, a deliberate distortion of the proper aims of social analysis? It is neither, for the following reasons. In an earlier stage of modern history the traditional theory (whose prototype for Horkheimer is Descartes' *Discourse on Method*) played a vital role in undermining stulti-

[4] For this and the immediately preceding passage see *KT II*, 193–194; see *KT I*, 168; and *Negations*, 141–142.

fied modes of thought and in opening up new possibilities for the human mastery of nature. Although philosophers such as Bacon and Descartes clearly expressed their hopes that social progress would result from the new foundations of knowledge, they could not show how these hopes were intrinsically related to the new methods, and thus the former remained extrinsic vis-à-vis the latter. But this fact is an objective condition of the prevailing social reality, not a theoretical lacuna, for the actual circumstances under which the satisfaction of essential needs for all men might be possible were not yet apparent. By the nineteenth century, however, the real basis for this possibility had been established, and it was then that the critical theory (and the social program of the oppressed) demanded that this possibility be realized through a rational form of production. The commitment to this demand is thus not arbitrary, but rather is based upon real historical possibilities.

Although it may now be conceded that the commitment itself is not arbitrary, it may yet be objected that such a commitment is extraneous as far as social analysis is concerned and that, while salutory in itself, it might serve to distort the analysis. Certainly it may do so in particular cases: The theory is not a magic wand in any sense. But can it really be extraneous? Any adequate study of present-day society should be able to delineate three aspects of the social reality. Represented schematically, these are: (1) the precise way in which the established set of institutions functions; (2) the present possibilities for a transition to a more rational set of institutions (one which would bring an end to war, injustice, poverty, and oppression); (3) the present possibilities for increased barbarism, intensified oppression, and thermonuclear annihilation. Obviously the elementary common interest of the human race is embodied in the second of these three aspects, and thus it represents

79

what we most need to know as a result of our analysis of society. But since the established set of institutions *already contains* the possibilities listed under (2) and (3), in fact one cannot even fully comprehend what "is" without also delineating what "can be" (and what ought to be). The actual incorporates the potential as part of its own structure. The prevailing reality always represents the realization of certain potentialities and the suppression of others, but the tension between the two sets is a permanent feature of the reality and is the driving force of historical change.

Far from being formally extraneous, then, an interest in (and *a fortiori* a commitment to, I should think) the possible rational organization of society is a necessary ingredient in the study of contemporary society. The results of any such study can be and should be examined from the point of view of what conclusions may be drawn regarding this possibility. The concepts and methodology employed in the study must be scrutinized in order to determine whether they are adequate for the complex task of uncovering the dynamic tension which unites the established order and the underlying conditions which form the basis for transcending it. Critical theory defines itself as the theory explicitly focussed on this task.

Marcuse's essay, "Philosophy and Critical Theory," describes in concrete terms what has been outlined above. The theory is oriented toward both the past and the future. With respect to the former, "critical theory concerns itself with preventing the loss of the truths which past knowledge labored to attain." And this is a necessary undertaking: "Reason, mind, morality, knowledge, and happiness are not only categories of bourgeois philosophy, but concerns of mankind. As such they must be preserved, if not derived anew." Under historical conditions which seemed hopelessly at variance with its assertions, earlier thought had

80

advanced the revolutionary propositions that (to take a few examples) rationality was a universal characteristic of men, that society ought to be reformed according to the potentialities of human rationality, and that freedom and rationality must necessarily be united. Yet the meaning of these earlier achievements is subject to great controversy, as is shown very clearly in the currently fashionable treatment of Plato, Rousseau, and Hegel—all of whom advanced one or more of these propositions—as "totalitarian" theorists.

Precisely in order to preserve the achievements of the past, theory must continually reinterpret and concretize them in the light of present possibilities. This is the second aspect of the twofold orientation of critical theory: "In the theoretical reconstruction of the social process, the critique of current conditions and the analysis of their tendencies necessarily include future-oriented components."[5] Specifically, the theory seeks to identify factors in the social organization of production, in technological developments, and in the consciousness of the majority which constitute a possible basis for a radically different society. At that point in history when the ancient design of freedom and happiness for the first time can be linked with a productive process adequate for the realization of this design on a universal scale, the theory of society must develop a schema that delineates the conditions under which the transition to the desired goal might be accomplished. The acceptance of this task determines the choice and significance of the basic concepts employed in the theory: "The Marxian categories class, exploitation, surplus value, profit, impoverishment, and breakdown are moments of a conceptual whole whose meaning is to be sought not in the reproduction of the

[5] This and the two preceding quotations are from *Negations,* 152, 147, 145.

present society, but in its transformation toward a just society" (*KT II,* 167).

This is the orientation of critical theory. And if it has one outstanding principle that is characteristic of its approach, it is that the concepts employed in theoretical analysis are an integral part of the reality which they seek to grasp—and thus that these concepts both help to change the reality and are themselves modified in the course of this change. This is the nature of dialectical thought, according to Horkheimer, as it is expressed in critical theory. "Dialectic . . . has incorporated in itself the fact that it is integrated in history. It knows its own concepts as moments of the historical constellation as well as the expression of that striving toward a just society that manifests itself differently both theoretically and practically in different historical situations and that at the same time preserves its identity" (*ibid.,* xi). In my own view nothing more clearly distinguishes critical theory from the predominant modes of social-science research than this principle, namely, that the theoretical analysis of the social process and the concepts employed therein, as an integral part of that process, are "self-reflexive." In other words, the theoretical analysis, inasmuch as it describes its "object" (the social process) accurately, thereby effects a change in the prevailing situation by uncovering and clarifying the possibilities for a transition to a just society; and simultaneously this change transforms the basis of the theoretical analysis itself by specifying more concretely the content of the concepts, such as freedom and happiness, with which it works.

Writing in the *Zeitschrift für Sozialforschung* for 1932, Horkheimer indicated specifically what tasks he hoped would be undertaken in the journal which he edited: an attempt to unify into a coherent whole the contributions of the various sections of the modern social sciences; the development of an adequate theoretical and empirical framework for social psychology; and the demonstration of the necessity for a thorough connection between the investigation of present society and the prospects for a radically different society in the future.[6] In the essay on critical theory which he wrote for the *Zeitschrift* in 1937, Marcuse suggested three reasons why the theory had to be newly applied and developed in the contemporary period. First, bourgeois society had entered a new phase in the twentieth century, that of authoritarianism and totalitarianism, and it was necessary to comprehend this phenomenon on the basis of the earlier history of bourgeois society. Second, the beginnings of the deliberate construction of socialism in parts of the world and the rising standard of living in Western capitalist society required a re-investigation of the goals of the struggle for liberation. And third, the specific content of those goals had to undergo modification in the process of "bringing to consciousness potentialities that have emerged within the maturing historical situation" (*Negations,* 158).

An example of the treatment of a specific problem will illustrate how Horkheimer, Marcuse, and their co-workers utilized the conception of critical theory outlined above. Perhaps the best example of all is the analysis of "materialism" found in two of Horkheimer's essays, "Materialismus und Metaphysik" and "Materialismus und Moral" (both published in 1933), and in Marcuse's "Philosophy and Critical Theory" and "On Hedonism." Historically, materialism had been opposed to "idealism" in two respects: (1) in asserting irreconcilable claims about the fundamental nature of reality (that is, Being); (2) in attitudes toward pleasure and happiness. Horkheimer and

[6] Passage quoted in Alfred Schmidt, "Nachwort des Herausgebers: Zur Idee der kritischen Theorie," *KT II,* 341–342.

Marcuse point out that both materialism and idealism share a common fault with respect to the first point, in that both hypostasize a particular principle and both invest "Being" with ethical overtones, identifying the highest reality with perfection. They argue that critical theory is a materialist theory not in this traditional sense, but only in its thorough-going concern with human happiness, its conviction that the achievement of happiness requires a transformation of the relations of production, and its opposition to the persistent attempts to identify the "essence" of man with some supra-historical "spiritual" qualities. Horkheimer emphatically contends that Marx's materialist theory is no "metaphysics of history."[7]

For them the tradition of idealism was correct in oppos-ing the hedonistic aspect of earlier materialism in the name of human progress: the discipline of labor and the disciplin-ing of the human appetitive functions were necessary stages in human liberation. But idealism's hidden side was a kind of "bad materialism," in the sense that empirical reality was consigned to a lower order of Being while contradictions were resolved in the realm of *Geist*. As a result, its own principles forced it beyond the scheme it sought to estab-lish. Horkheimer uses the example of Kant's categorical imperative (*KT I*, 82): Since the isolated individual who is the subject of the categorical imperative cannot realize his demands in the empirical reality, he is driven to change that reality (the social order) in order to establish the pos-sibility for its realization. The materialism of critical theory preserves this element of idealism, namely, that its practice must be guided by concepts which retain an aspect of abstractness so long as the desired goal has not yet been reached (*Negations*, 153).

[7] *KT I*, 105; see 19, 46; and Schmidt, 347–350.

II

The limitations of critical theory had been indicated at the outset. The fact that this theory is an integral part of the ongoing historical struggle for a rational set of social institutions means that the dispute over its correct conception and application has an objective basis in the changing social situation and that this dispute will persist as long as the struggle itself (*KT II*, 189). Thus there is no way in which the theory can provide a definitive and permanent portrait of the social process; and its claim that this short-coming reflects an objective condition, rather than a failure stemming from a distorted conceptual framework, cannot be conclusively demonstrated in the theory. The theory insists that the concepts employed in the analysis of the social process must embody a determinate possibility—namely, that men can organize their social relations in such a way as to eliminate war, poverty, injustice, and oppression—as a *real* possibility of the present; but it cannot prove that this possibility *must* be realized. In this sense only the realization of this possibility can demonstrate the "correctness" of the theory.

This internal limitation within the theory, the fact that it is necessarily bound at every particular point to the concrete historical situation, affects the way in which not only the nineteenth-century heritage, but even the relatively recent contributions of the Frankfurt group in the nineteen-thirties, must be approached today. Both Horkheimer and Marcuse have emphasized this principle in the last few years upon the occasion of the republication of their earlier essays.[8] They insist that these essays no longer have the

[8] References for this discussion are: *Negations*, xi–xx; *KT I*, ix–xiv; and *II*, vii–xi. Since these are brief pieces, no page references will be given for the quotations drawn from them.

same significance as before. With reference to these essays Marcuse notes that "no revision could bridge the chasm that separates the period in which they were written from the present one," and of the perspective which unites them he says: "What was correct in it has since become, perhaps not false, but a thing of the past." Horkheimer maintains that "thoughtless and dogmatic application of critical theory to practice in the changed historical reality would only serve to hasten the process which it had denounced," and he makes it clear that he is referring also to the present meaning of his own earlier work. In assisting the relevance of critical theory for the present tasks of social change and social science, therefore, we must try to understand precisely what has happened in the interim.

The explanation seems to be quite simple. The assumption of power by the proletariat in important sectors of the highly developed capitalist society seemed to be a reasonable expectation throughout the first half of the twentieth century. To this traditional vision of Marxian theory had been added the special urgency of immediately transcending the barbaric phase of capitalism which had revealed itself in European fascism. It appeared that the oppositional forces had sufficiently matured so that the struggle against fascism could be carried over directly into the construction of democratic socialism in some of the technically advanced nations. Not only was their expectation disappointed: the prevailing social situation changed dramatically with the "integration" of the proletariat in bourgeois society. That this may be a "temporary" phenomenon is quite possible; but, as Horkheimer remarks elsewhere, what is involved is the agony of generations of human beings (is it necessary to refer to the fate of the Vietnamese and other peoples?). The new phase of bourgeois society is characterized above all by the management and control of behavior in all aspects of social existence exercised through a myriad of manipulative techniques.

What is the impact of this new phase on the situation of critical theory? In Horkheimer's words, "thought and will, theoretical and practical reason, are no longer united." For Marcuse it means that the theory cannot now hope to "take hold of the masses." These statements strongly imply that the expectation outlined in the preceding paragraph exerted a determining influence upon the conception and structure of the essays written in the nineteen-thirties. And indeed they show such an influence clearly. The contradictions of bourgeois society, as they are expressed both in the productive process and in cultural forms, are analyzed in these essays not abstractly, not in the light of a fully elaborated ideal of socialism, but rather from the perspective of the then-existing possibilities for the initiation of the transition to socialism, most importantly the possibility of bringing the productive process under the control of a rational plan through the activity of the organized proletariat.

At that time a formidable new obstacle blocking the path of this transition had arisen: the terrorism and barbarism of the fascist movement. Theory could aid in the struggle against fascism by understanding its relationship to the earlier stages of bourgeois society, the factors responsible for its popular success, and the inner contradictions peculiar to it. The Frankfurt group, following the lead of Lukács' *Geschichte und Klassenbewusstsein* (especially the analysis of the "antinomies of bourgeois thought"), concentrated on tracing the contradictions expressed in cultural forms— particularly the history of philosophy—in order to discover to what extent intellectual culture had assisted the rise of fascism by preparing "its own liquidation." In other words,

87

they sought to uncover the factors in the cultural inheritance of the present which had pre-formed the consciousness of large segments of the developed bourgeois society in such a way that the society as a whole could fall victim to the depravities of totalitarian barbarism.

I think it will now be clear what Marcuse means in saying that what was correct in the theory is "a thing of the past." A reading of the essays will disclose that they contain many profound insights into the problems to which they were addressed; these insights unquestionably possess enduring value. They succeed—often brilliantly—in partially explaining the preparation for the fascist stage of bourgeois society. But the overriding problems have changed, and thus the correctness of the earlier theory cannot suffice for the present. Since the theory cannot at the moment work within the framework of an expectation of the assumption of power by the proletariat in the traditional sense, and since this group remains the only *social class* appropriate for the task of radical social change (as the *Essay on Liberation* clearly affirms), theory at present will necessarily appear more "abstract" than before. In accordance with changes in the objective social situation, it must confront precisely those tendencies which have blunted the sources of radical political action, namely, the growing apparatus of manipulation and control.

But this is not the whole story. The recent activities of the Frankfurt group reveal differences among them which find expression both theoretically and practically, and these differences reflect alternative ways of applying the heritage of critical theory now. Those presently identified with the Institute's affairs in Frankfurt (Jürgen Habermas and, until recently, Theodor Adorno) have repeatedly requested police protection for the Institute in response to threats and pressures from radical students; among other things, the students have painted slogans on the walls of the Institute's building drawn from the radical pamphlets which Horkheimer authored during the nineteen-thirties under the pseudonym "Heinrich Regius." In general Marcuse has been much more in sympathy with the radical student movement, although certainly he has not adopted an uncritical attitude toward it. More significantly, opposition to the American actions in Vietnam became an important part of Marcuse's work during the last few years, and he has affirmed that the spirit of those social forces with whose fate the critical theory was intertwined, the spirit which experienced its last great moment on the European continent in the Spanish Civil War, is now expressed in the anti-imperialist struggle in the Third World.[9] By way of contrast, even allowing for the fact that they live outside the United States (for so do Jean-Paul Sartre and Bertrand Russell), Marcuse's colleagues among the Frankfurt group have been remarkably reticent and supercilious with respect to Vietnam.[10]

In 1968 Horkheimer described thusly the situation and tasks of critical theory (*KT I*, xiii):

To measure the so-called free world according to its own concept, to treat it critically and nevertheless to take up the defense of its ideas against Hitlerian, Stalinist or other variations of fascism, is the right and duty of everyone who thinks. In spite of its ominous potential and of all injustice both internal and external, the free world still constitutes at the moment an island in space and time whose end in the ocean of despotism would also signify the end of the culture to which the critical theory still belongs.

---

[9] *Negations*, xv, 269.
[10] There is much more that could be detailed concerning these practical differences. In addition, Habermas and Schmidt have published critiques of Marcuse's work. An independent exploration of this subject would be valuable for contemporary radicalism.

What are we to gather from this, apart from a feeling of gratitude that we do not all have to practice critical theory under conditions similar to those which the Vietnamese must endure? Horkheimer also warns the left (*ibid.*, xii) that it is "pseudo-revolutionary" to encourage the constant possibility of a breakdown of democracy into totalitarianism, and presumably he is referring to attacks on the universities, the press, the courts, and so forth. Are we to conclude from this that only liberal reform activity will be blessed with the sanction of a chastened critical theory?

It seems, then, we are to carry on the analyses begun by the earlier critical theory after having excised the element of active involvement with the forces of radical social change which permeated the conception of this theory in the nineteen-thirties. Alfred Schmidt even suggests a program for us: problems explored in the earlier period which represent fruitful areas of investigation for the present are the structure of history, the contradiction between idealism and materialism, and the contrast between critical and traditional theory (*op. cit.*, 343). Schmidt has published an impressive number of books and essays in the last decade which, together with the writings of Adorno, illustrate the orientation of critical theory in Frankfurt during recent times. In addition, we have the examples of Horkheimer's later work which are collected in the volume entitled *Zur Kritik der instrumentellen Vernunft*.

They remain exceedingly competent writings, to be sure, and not at all unimportant; yet in so many of these recent contributions the cutting edge of the earlier theory is missing. The explanation is to be found, I think, in the fact that the contemporary theory has not been related concretely to its social situation; it is this circumstance, rather than the fact that the theory and its practitioners have become academically respectable, which decisively separates it from its preceding stage in the nineteen-thirties and -forties. Horkheimer has described the changed conditions of bourgeois society and has explained that the earlier essays are permeated with economic and political conceptions that are no longer "immediately valid," but his explanation is incomplete in at least two respects: (1) it does not indicate what shortcomings in the earlier theory itself, apart from the altered social situation, were responsible for this loss of validity; and (2) it does not even attempt to ask whether there are any contemporary forms of radical political action which are linked with the concerns of critical theory.

Marcuse has confronted both of these issues, and to a great extent this explains the differences between him and other members of the Frankfurt group over the contemporary orientation of critical theory. In the Preface to *Negations* and in the essay "The Obsolescence of Marxism?"[11] he argues that the conceptions of the earlier theory, both in the nineteenth and twentieth centuries, were "not radical enough." These conceptions did not comprehend the possibility that a late stage of capitalism could stabilize itself for an extended period during which (within the small circle of technically advanced nations) a comparatively high standard of living for the population as a whole, and the concomitant management of opinion and behavior, could suppress the contradictions inherent in the productive process. Likewise there were defects in the representation of socialism arising out of the fact that the tasks of socialism had been outlined with regard to a stage of capitalism that had been transcended. Finally, the especially complex problem of the transition from capitalism to socialism has to be re-thought in light of these factors. In sum, the theory

---

[11] In Nicholas Lobkowicz, ed., *Marx and the Western World* (Notre Dame: University of Notre Dame Press, 1967), 409–417.

was not utopian enough on the one hand, in that it did not foresee the possibilities opened up by high productivity and shortened labor-time within an advanced stage of capitalism; on the other hand, it had not been broad enough to encompass the difficulties involved in building socialism in economically backward areas under the constant threat of war.

As far as the second issue is concerned, it seems to me that among the contributions to critical theory only Marcuse's recent writings have attempted to connect the heritage of the theory with the immensely difficult task of discovering modes of radical political action appropriate to the latest configurations of bourgeois society. This is true especially of the article "Repressive Tolerance" and the book *An Essay on Liberation*. The proponents of critical theory unanimously agree that the present stage of capitalism is marked by these two distinctive features, among others: (1) the gradual integration of all facets of social and cultural life (for example, sexuality) as instruments of control over individual behavior; and (2) the development of increasingly sophisticated techniques for the management and manipulation of behavior. Under such circumstances opposition to the system, cut off from a mass base in the working class and presented to the public consciousness by the "communications" media in thoroughly distorted forms, must employ strategies which necessarily have little in common with those of the past.

"Repressive Tolerance" and *An Essay on Liberation* examine some of those strategies and the social context in which they have been developed. The former explores the underlying basis for the transformation of the social function of the traditional civil liberties: In a society characterized by pervasive manipulation from above, the preformation of consciousness and the control of mass communications severely limit the extent to which the "free exchange of ideas" and "rational discourse" can serve as elements of the decision-making process. This essay has been a vital factor, for example, in widespread discussions concerning attitudes toward campus recruitment by the military services and by corporations conspicuously involved in war production. The remarks on the uses of obscenity and on the novel aspects of the French uprising in May 1968 in *An Essay on Liberation* are also indicative of the way in which Marcuse has continually striven to relate the comprehensive picture of the social process offered by critical theory to currently existing and emerging forms of opposition, no matter how fragmented, disorganized, or hopeless they may seem at the moment.

The lesson appears obvious: Divorced from an intense concern with the ongoing active forms of opposition, critical theory loses its distinctive characteristic and assumes a regular position within the academic (and social) division of labor. Its progress is not assured solely by virtue of the fact that homage is rendered to it in an increasing number of elegant philosophical and sociological exercises. Its only unique value consists in whatever ability it possesses at any moment to sharpen the existing social contradictions by depicting the conditions constituting the gap between the prevailing situation and the possible rational organization of humane society.

III

Within the established academic ranks one must expect to meet with gallant resistance to the notions that the intellectual's task is to sharpen social contradictions and that the analytical concepts of social science must be able to reveal the hidden potentialities and trends of the present. One cannot hope that an essay on critical theory or any other merely ratiocinative devices would prompt many defections. Yet the critical theory claims no monopoly of truth and disdains no insights that may be gleaned even from the remains of respectable scholarship. The "scientific study of society" which has as its objective radical social change begins its contemporary theoretical and practical work with the knowledge of its inability to limn the co-ordinates of action that would bridge the gap between what is and what should be. An element of abstractness is thus imposed upon it, but its central question is fully concrete: What are the connections between the existing oppositional forces and the internal social contradictions peculiar to the present stage of capitalism?

The value and potential of any particular oppositional movement depends upon the degree to which its programs and tendencies confront the system at its "leading edges," that is, in terms of the newest features of the system's struggle for survival. In fact the failure to do so can be not only unfortunate, but disastrous: the best illustration is the European Left's blindness—until it was much too late—to the real danger of fascism. Despite its ostensible defeat, fascism served capitalist society by destroying the militant European proletariat precisely at the time when economic crises might have paved the way for an assumption of power by the proletariat in the traditional sense. A return to the forms of struggle of the pre-fascist era is extremely unlikely, and in order to avoid tilting at windmills the opposition must continually search for new ground upon which to make its stand. The apparently undisciplined and amorphous character of the radical opposition in the advanced capitalist nations at present is good evidence of this "testing" phase of its development.

The pressure of events in the years since the Second World War has forced a recognition (in both the theory and practice of the radical opposition) of the fact that the domestic and the international arenas of conflict are interconnected. To a certain extent class conflict has been internationalized; the "wretched of the earth" in the Third World have taken up the struggle formerly waged by the domestic European and North American proletariat. The response of the ruling interests has been perfectly true to form: the barbarism and terror which fascism unleashed both internally and externally in the earlier period now operates exclusively against the underdeveloped world, as in Algeria and Vietnam. Moreover, this campaign against the non-white, pre-industrialized peoples strengthens the hegemony of the ruling interests in the developed nations by keeping the terrifying visage of the *Untermenschen* in the popular consciousness. And yet, despite the most ruthless attempts at suppression from without, various forms of socialism have become the authentic instrument of social progress in the Third World.

Until now the critical theory has not come to terms adequately with these trends. As far as the developed nations are concerned, the full impact of the anti-imperialist struggle on the stabilized position of the domestic proletariat (and vice versa) is not yet clear. It is possible that the remoteness of the actual conflicts and other factors such as racism will prevent the anti-imperialist uprising from becoming a decisive element of social conflict in the advanced capitalist nations for a long time; but there can be no doubt that the increasing pressure on the empire's frontiers is a crucial feature of its over-all dilemma. With reference to the development of socialism in the economically backward areas,

. . . there is the possibility of skipping the stage of repressive capitalist industrialization, an industrialization that has led to increasingly more powerful domination of the productive and distributive apparatus over the underlying population. Instead the backward countries may have the chance for a technological development which keeps the industrial apparatus in line with the vital needs and freely developing faculties of human beings.[12]

Should this possibility be realized even in the smallest measure, there would be profound consequences for the future of socialism in the advanced nations. Thus the critical theory must regularly review the concepts with which it approaches present-day society in the light of events in the new socialist countries, especially China and Cuba.

The overriding obstacle to the development of a radical opposition on a mass basis in contemporary capitalist society is, according to the analysis of critical theory, the pervasive manipulation of consciousness. This fact pertains to the material basis of the society, and not merely to the "superstructure," because the management of needs is an essential feature of the productive process itself. The manipulation of behavior and of the expression of needs is the determinate framework within which the integration of the traditional working class as full members of the capitalist consumer system has taken place. This is the second major problematic (the first, as described above, is the interaction of internal and external opposition) confronting critical theory today: It must uncover the dialectic of this integration, the process by which new contradictions arise as some of the old are repressed. Some aspects of this dialectic are already apparent, for example the fact that, as the whole population is drawn fully into the complex network of commodities and as the range of available

12 "The Obsolescence of Marxism," 415. See the "Political Preface 1966" to *Eros and Civilization* (2nd ed.; Boston: Beacon, 1966).

products expands to immense proportions, the character of the expected benefits and satisfactions to be derived from the use of these products changes decisively. First, the products are increasingly tailored for psychologically based wants; and second, the promised satisfactions are progressively inflated beyond all possibility of realization. The average consumer is led to believe that these seemingly commonplace items will satiate his wildest fantasies. The overt cynicism toward these messages is only one aspect of the reaction to them, for there is sufficient evidence to show that an increasing range of unfulfilled expectations is developed, mostly on the subconscious level.

The products supplied cannot, under any circumstances, really gratify these expectations. Thus a fund of suppressed resentment accumulates which finds an outlet in diffused aggressiveness: behavior in the driving of automobiles is only the most obvious example of this. There is, therefore, an inherent instability built into the expanding consumer society that must—according to the necessities of the system itself—increase, and probably at an increasing rate. (There may also be a concomitant "natural" limit to the manipulation of wants, although this has not yet been worked out.) The growing dissatisfaction with the false gratifications embodied in consumer products *could,* in connection with other factors, provide the basis, among the majority of the population, for the transition to a system of unmanipulated and "real" gratification. It provides the possibility of linking up broad strata of the population with those aspects of the current opposition directed against the perversion of needs and gratification in the consumer society. Free distribution of necessities ("free stores," public food kitchens, and so forth), collective activity which lowers the level of individual material needs, and sheer indifference to the garish wares hawked in the marketplace

97

are some of the present practices which show every sign of spreading rapidly.

This activity of the opposition is not merely opposition, but also the affirmation of a qualitatively different mode of social arrangements. It affirms, as against the system's postponement of real leisure and gratification, as against the system's perpetuation of inhuman labor in the service of endlessly expanding false needs, the right to enjoy a rational set of material necessities on the basis of the minimum labor possible in light of present technological capabilities. The tyranny of false needs and unnecessary labor must be overthrown *in the individuals,* as a precondition for liberation. Marcuse's *Essay on Liberation* amplifies the apparently paradoxical thesis that was stated in *One-Dimensional Man,* namely, that individuals must be free for their liberation, that is, that a decisive break with the "continuum of domination" must occur in the course of the struggle against the present forms of domination. Technological capabilities have already made possible the abolition of material scarcity, and thus the opposition to the manipulation of needs is critical: For the attempt to shape the innermost drives of the individual threatens to preserve the continuum of domination just as the possibility for the real gratification of basic needs has emerged.

The attempted manipulation of the individual's psychological dynamic (on a mass basis), which has been intensified steadily since the First World War, is directly related to the dramatic technological innovations occurring in the same period. The means for overcoming the traditional material obstacles to human happiness, and the means for perpetuating misery and unhappiness through a prodigious waste of human and natural resources, have increased in the same proportions; more correctly, these seemingly contradictory tendencies have been gradually intermingling. This syndrome presents critical theory with a third important problematic. It is not enough to say that the process of mastering nature through technological innovation must itself be mastered, that a turn from quantitative to qualitative technical progress is required: One should not underestimate the immensity of the effort which will be required in order to relieve modern technology of the burden of its attachment to the structure of domination. *How* this technology is to be liberated is the decisive question.

The structure of manipulation in advanced capitalism is displayed in the division of internal and external opposition (the apparent conflict of interest between the working class in the West and in the Third World), in the more "democratic" access to a fraudulent consumer market, and in the inability of the society to control an increasingly more destructive and wasteful technological apparatus. To analyze this structure concretely we must ask: (1) What is the actual state of manipulation at present? For example, has the distinction between "real" needs and "false" needs been eliminated or effectively suppressed? (2) What prospects now exist for the refinement and intensification of the manipulative framework? (3) What actual counter-tendencies are evident which might encourage the hope that a breakdown of this framework would have positive consequences? In other words, what features of the internal contradictions in the manipulative apparatus could pave the way for the emergence of free individuals—individuals who determine their own needs?

The very intensity of the process of management and manipulation, the necessity for the constant supervision in the realm of consciousness, is the best evidence of the essential fragility of the social structure which requires it. It is not the potential breakdown of that structure in an abstract sense that is of interest to the radical opposition, however, but rather the specific conditions of breakdown. The extension of terror and barbarism from the foreign lands, where it is presently confined, to the domestic front is a permanent possibility. Already there is abundant evidence that the sustained effort at suppressing insurgency abroad will profoundly affect the political process at home. The radical opposition and critical theory have the twofold task of confronting the renewed threat of terror and of laying the basis for liberation.

On Sexuality and Politics
in the Work of Herbert Marcuse

JOHN DAVID OBER

Herbert Marcuse uniquely transgresses the current "traditional wisdom" of the mass media which by the end of the
decade of the sixties had in concert proclaimed the advent
of *the* sexual revolution in America. Those who announced
or participated in the upheaval and its commercial institutionalization tend to split into two camps: those who
deplore the collapse of traditional Christian codes of conduct and those who applaud and help to create the supposed emancipation from the older verities.

Marcuse belongs to neither camp. He has always been
the foe of the hair-brained enthusiasts who have tried to
impose sexual codes of conduct on others in the name of
transcendental ethical systems, especially those who invade
the realm of privacy in their efforts to unmask and de-
nounce carnal pleasure as sin. One of the most repressive
features of Western culture has been the long-established
dualism of the spirit and the flesh.[1] But Marcuse is no
less the foe of all who reduce the definition of human

[1] See the comments of Thomas Nagel, "Sexual Perversion," *Journal
of Philosophy*, LXVI, no. 1 (January 16, 1969), 12–13. Also Herbert
Marcuse, *Eros and Civilization* (Boston: Beacon, 1955), 210–211.

liberation to the dimension of pure sexuality, a reduction which leads in the end to the simplistic equation that unhampered sexual intercourse (on- or off-stage, in public or private) is identical with freedom. Not unlike the erstwhile Christian moralists, the advocates of sexual reductionism (especially scientists with calipers and computers) establish and disseminate information about normative standards and techniques which may serve to replace the old taboos with more stringent codes of behavior against which the individual must match his own performance and "degree of liberation."

Marcuse has most frequently been misunderstood in his opposition to the implications of the so-called sexual revolution. His unique position among contemporary social critics consists in his rejection of both Puritan taboos and the wanton sexual abandon which emerged during the past decade. Marcuse's rejection of both previous restrictions and current sexual reductionism is neither self-contradictory nor utopian, neither a defense of libertinism nor a self-styled neo-puritanism.

What, then, is the source of the confusion? Apparently it lies in an unbridged gap between *Eros and Civilization* and *One-Dimensional Man,* in the unclear relationship between the concept "surplus-repression" in the former and the concept "repressive desublimation" in the latter. More precisely, "surplus-repression" would seem to conjure up the very sexual rebellion which is occurring against the lingering taboos in an effort to remove the surplus.[2] "Repressive desublimation" would seem, on the contrary, to

[2] One student informed me that Marcuse's views of sexual conduct had received their finest popular expression in "The Playboy Philosophy" of Hugh Hefner! See the discussion below. Also, see *The New York Times* of October 2, 1969, for Paul VI's amusing denunciation of Freud and Marcuse as advocates of "disgusting and unbridled expressions of eroticism."

imply a harsh condemnation of the recent sexual emancipation. Marcuse himself is aware of the scant treatment given the latter concept and of the resulting criticism that either he has modified his position between the two books or has unwittingly contradicted his earlier views. To date he has had no occasion to discuss the relationship between "surplus-repression" and "repressive desublimation," both of which play major roles in his general critique of advanced industrial society.

This study will attempt to explore the relationship between the two and to respond to the charge of inconsistency by demonstrating that the content of the sexual revolution is neither revolutionary nor liberating, but rather the extension and solidification of the most repressive features of advanced industrial society. To be sure, the new forms of domination and control operate within a broader and more lenient framework than the old. But in terms of the individual's psychological development, the decrease in both acknowledged and unacknowledged limitations on sexual behavior by no means demonstrates by itself that repression has declined or that mental health has improved. The sexual explosion does not herald the coming of the non-repressive, sublimated civilization envisaged in *Eros and Civilization*. On the contrary, the rampant commercialization, not only of sex, but of the sexual revolution itself, may well indicate an increase in the ability of the established society to tolerate more, and more divergent, forms of behavior because the shrinking of the human psyche and imagination by means of technological manipulation has rendered impotent such formerly dangerous forms of behavior.

Human freedom, for Marcuse, has always been and remains far more than a matter to be decided by individual opinion alone. The belief that thinking oneself to be free makes it so, reeks of ritual magic and is a regressive throw-back to the concept of "inner" freedom which arose during the early Reformation period. Similarly, freedom is more than the right to do anything one wants, especially if what one wants is contrary to the continuation of human civilization and is the result of the preconditioning of goals, desires, and beliefs. Freedom, even sexual freedom, is a question of politics, but a politics which transcends the accepted present and omnipresent situation in which the vote and the candidates are marketed and sold as proof of freedom.

No attempt to discuss Marcuse's theory of psychological development would be accurate if it failed to take into account the relationship between the individual personality and the socio-historical content embodied in the forces of socialization at the present time. And today more than ever, those forces are an amalgamation of political pressures operating for the preservation of the established powers. The interconnection between sexuality and politics at present reveals itself paradoxically as an increase in the toleration of divergent sexual behavior coupled with an increase in control over individual self-realization by utilizing that toleration. The release of libidinal energy continues to serve the interests of domination. And it is only political behavior which can undermine the existence and the need for the existence of institutions which convince men to participate in their own unfreedom while believing themselves to be free.

I

In the earlier of the two books Marcuse introduces the concepts "surplus-repression" and "performance principle" in order to clarify the ambiguity in the Freudian theory between biological, individual instinctual development and the historical vicissitudes of the instincts.[3] The specific institutions and values of a given society play a major role in accounting for variations in the socialization process from one society to another.

Freud defined repression operating within the individual as "a preliminary stage of condemnation, something between flight and condemnation."[4] In the course of psychosexual development repression arises, and can only arise, after the split between unconscious and conscious mental activity has occurred; for the role of repression is "simply in turning something away, and keeping it at a distance, from the conscious."[5] The fundamental result of repression is to transform instinctual pleasures into painful experiences which continue to be rejected from consciousness:

The fulfillment of these wishes would no longer produce an affect of pleasure, but one of pain; and it is just this conversion of affect that constitutes the essence of what we call "repression."[6]

Freud himself considered the discovery of repression together with the unmasking of infantile sexuality to be the two greatest achievements of psychoanalysis.[7]

For Freud, repression, and even growing repression, is an essential precondition for and an indigenous part of human civilization. But Marcuse argues—against the neo-Freudian revisionists—that there are passages in Freud

[3] Herbert Marcuse, *Eros and Civilization,* 35.
[4] Sigmund Freud, "Repression," *The Standard Edition of the Complete Psychological Works of Sigmund Freud XIV* (London: Hogarth, 1957), 146.
[5] *Ibid.,* 147.
[6] Sigmund Freud, "The Interpretation of Dreams," *The Basic Writings of Sigmund Freud* (New York: Random House, 1938), 537.
[7] Sigmund Freud, *On the History of the Psycho-Analytic Movement* (New York: Norton, 1966), 16.

which counteract Freud's own denial of the possibilities of a society without repression, or better, the reversal of the process of increasing repression.[8] And, indeed, if repression as an individual psychic phenomenon emerges only after or concurrently with the development of consciousness, then the term necessarily includes the social dimension, the institutions and agents of the socialization process. As Marcuse indicates, these institutions and agents are not mere abstractions; they are imbued with the specific content of a specific socio-economic set of arrangements. Freud's Reality Principle, therefore, is not a formal or reified structure which functions in the same way at all times and places in order to prepare individuals for their social roles in the conquest of scarcity in the struggle for existence. Different socio-economic systems socialize in qualitatively different ways.[9]

In order to clarify the fact that the specific content of the Reality Principle varies historically, Marcuse introduces his second concept, the "performance principle," which is defined as "the prevailing historical form of the *reality principle*."[10] For Marcuse, then, the concept of repression must be understood in its twofold dimensions: as a technical psychic mechanism of the individual to deny the entrance of painful instincts into consciousness; and as a social process which transforms libidinous energy into channels which are useful to the preservation and perpetuation of the on-going society. Neither Freud nor Marcuse would deny for an instant that throughout human history, it is repression which has made possible all human society by curtailing and transforming the polymorphously perverse

[8] Herbert Marcuse, *Eros and Civilization*, 5.

[9] Note the interesting examples cited by Karl Polanyi, *The Great Transformation* (Boston: Beacon, 1957), Chapter 4, 43ff.

[10] Herbert Marcuse, *Eros and Civilization*, 35.

sexual energy of the individual into sublimated, deflected activities through sublimation.

The historians of civilization seem to be unanimous in the opinion that such deflection of sexual motive powers from sexual aims to new aims, a process which merits the name of *sublimation,* has furnished powerful components for all cultural accomplishments. We will, therefore, add that the same process acts in the development of every individual . . .[11]

But is Marcuse justified in his assumption that in the work of Freud himself there is a socio-historical dimension which justifies the introduction of the concept "performance principle"? The justification can be seen only by elucidating the fundamental lack of clarity in certain aspects of Freud's own career and work. First, he always viewed himself as a scientist, a practicing physician, and not as a speculative philosopher or sociologist. "His political thought, accordingly, is neither systematically developed nor logically unified."[12] Second, his theories underwent almost constant re-working in the light of new evidence acquired in the course of his practice.[13] Third, in spite of the difficulties in piecing together a complete socio-political theory from Freud's writings, Roazen has shown effectively that Freud ". . . was not as insensitive to historical change as some seem to assume."[14] For example, on occasion Freud comments on the changes in mental health and illness wrought

[11] Sigmund Freud, "Three Contributions to the Theory of Sex," *The Basic Writings of Sigmund Freud,* 584.

[12] Thomas Johnston, *Freud and Political Thought* (New York: Citadel, 1965), 15.

[13] Paul Roazen, *Freud: Political and Social Thought* (New York: Knopf, 1968), Chapter II, 76ff. According to Roazen, "Freud was not a comprehensive thinker; as he said in a letter to Groddeck, 'I have a special talent for being satisfied with a fragment'" (p. 87). How is it possible to write a book on Freud's political and social theories without a single mention of Marcuse's work?

[14] *Ibid.,* 266.

by historical changes in the specific values of society.[15] In his paper of 1908, " 'Civilized' Sexual Morality and Modern Nervous Illness," Freud launches a virulent attack on the "spread of modern nervous illness" due to the fact that "the demands made on the efficiency of the individual in the struggle for existence have greatly increased and it is only by putting out all his mental powers that he can meet them." The increase in nervous illness and the emergence of new forms of mental illness under established technological arrangements are exacerbated by the stringent and unmanageable sexual restrictions imposed by the ethical norms of Victorianism; the demands of the specific civilization lead to a curtailment of behavior which surpasses the limits of human endurance.

In addition, Freud distinguishes three historical stages in the evolution of the sexual instinct in culture. The three move from the free exercise of the instinct without regard to the aims of reproduction to "present-day 'civilized' sexual morality," in which all of the sexual instinct is suppressed except what serves the aim of *"legitimate* reproduction."[16] Here is an example of "surplus-repression": the subordination of excessive amounts of libidinal energy to *specific* laws, customs, and institutions—laws, customs, and institutions which may subvert freedom through external aggression and by extracting too great a toll from the resources of the individual. As envisaged by Marcuse, the reversal of the process of increasing surplus-repression would not mean the collapse of civilization into barbarism, but the transformation of an overly demanding form of civilization into one which recognizes the instinctual needs of men as well as the limits of human tolerance in terms

[15] *Ibid.*

[16] Sigmund Freud, " 'Civilized' Sexual Morality and Modern Nervous Illness," in *The Standard Edition IX* (London: Hogarth, 1959), 189. Italics in the original.

of repression. By analogy, one might say that Marcuse has added the fully developed social dimension to the Freudian theory in much the same way that Locke introduced the concept of society into the theory of Hobbes. For Hobbes, the successful attack upon sovereignty destroys the contract and hurls man back into anarchy; for Locke, the leaders and even the form of the government can be changed without destroying civilization. But the theory presupposes the existence of autonomous individuals and thereby reveals itself as belonging to the pre-industrial period. Similarly, the society of which Freud was a part differed radically from the one which emerged from the dust and trenches of the First World War.

In that pre-War stage of historical development the suppression and control of sexuality was still achieved by means of moral and legalistic prohibitions and by rigidly defining and causing the introjection of the accepted channels of "legitimate" sexuality. The rules were enforced by religious and legal disapprobation against all deviance. To be sure, Freud argued that such narrow limits produce neurosis by imposing demands upon the individual which he cannot meet in health. The result of such "surplus-repression" was the sublimation of the sexual instincts beyond the human capacity for sublimation,[17] and the perpetuation of a particular society with its repressive performance principle at the expense of the health and relative happiness of the individual. For Marcuse, as we shall see, the repression continues today; but it is created and reinforced by the new dynamic of advanced industrial society.

[17] Freud illustrated the limits of toleration to the suppression of sexuality at the end of his Clark University lectures with the fable of the Schilda horse which died when underfed for reasons of economy. See *The Standard Edition XI* (London: Hogarth, 1957), 54.

109

Many other instances of Freud's awareness of the importance of specific social institutions, values, and relationships can be found, together with his condemnation of societies which extract too much by means of repression. In *Civilization and Its Discontents* he remarks that it is "unquestionable that an actual change in men's attitudes to property" would help to lessen the threat of aggression and enhance human happiness to some degree.[18] Nor did Freud believe that fundamental social change was impossible. He was much too aware of the importance of socio-historical changes upon the development of the individual psyche in the past to ignore the possibilities for future changes. The principal problem with Freud's historical thought, according to Roazen, is that "he was tempted to construct historical stages on scanty evidence . . . Ultimately, he was more interested in illustrating timeless truths than in learning about unique historical developments."[19]

Surplus-repression for Marcuse is repression over and above that required for the continuation of the human race in civilization. It is "the restrictions necessitated by social domination; these additional controls arising from specific institutions of domination are what we denote as *surplus-repression*." And there have been various modes of domination which result in various historical forms of the Reality Principle.[20] The relationships of any given society form a constellation which gives that society an identifiable character; and the values of that society, values which obviously figure in the socialization process, reflect the

[18] Sigmund Freud, *Civilization and Its Discontents* (Garden City: Doubleday), 103.
[19] Paul Roazen, *op. cit.*, 266.
[20] Herbert Marcuse, *Eros and Civilization*, 35 and 37.

institutional arrangements of the society as a whole.[21] A given institution or value can only be understood in terms of the whole, and social change necessarily involves a change in the whole constellation.

In the paper " 'Civilized' Sexual Morality," Freud reiterates a constant theme that the retardation and suppression of sexual development and behavior (functions which are performed by the agents of socialization—parents, educational institutions, religious institutions) are necessary not only to the survival of civilization, but also to the perpetuation of the specific form of civilization in which socio-economic arrangements permit the young of "the educated classes" to attain independence and earn a living only after twenty or more years of life. Sexual repression works in the service of a specific form of social and economic dependence:

This reminds one, incidentally, of the intimate interconnection between all our cultural institutions and of the difficulty of altering any part of them without regard to the whole.[22]

Freud expresses the same view even more strongly at the conclusion of his paper, "The Sexual Enlightenment of Children." He praises the growth of secular education against church-dominated instruction, but notes the critical omission of sexual enlightenment even among the former. Authentic enlightenment, change, emancipation can never result from isolated instances of revision and reform:

Here, once again, we see the unwisdom of sewing a single silk patch on to a tattered coat—the impossibility of carrying out an

[21] See Herbert Marcuse, "A Note on Dialectic," *Reason and Revolution* (Boston: Beacon, 1960), vii–xvi.

[22] Sigmund Freud, " 'Civilized' Sexual Morality and Modern Nervous Illness," *The Standard Edition IX,* 196.

111

isolated reform without altering the foundations of the whole system.[23]

The preceding discussion attempted to demonstrate that there are legitimate reasons for assuming that the seeds of a socio-political critique of contemporary forms of civilization exist within the works of Freud himself, in spite of ambiguities in his theory between the permanent elements of the psyche and the historical vicissitudes they have undergone and will surely continue to undergo.

Eros and Civilization is first and foremost an attempt to present the possibilities and processes for the removal of surplus-repression by the radical transformation of a society whose continued existence necessitates such repression, regardless of the specific agents of repression. It becomes increasingly clear that the not-so-civilized domination exercised by the technological father is replacing the domination exercised by the "civilized" morality of the Victorian father. But indications abound that the change in the agents and even the dynamic of socialization has not changed the performance principle and has not, therefore, led to the decline in surplus-repression. The Freudian analysis stands vindicated once again: the growth of material and technological progress continues hand in hand with the growth of repression under the performance principle of advanced industrial society.[24] And the truth of the Freudian analysis is the condemnation of a society whose governing principle is the excessive utilization of libidinal energy for preconceived social projects, many of which curtail the imagination, destroy the well-springs of human relationships, and negate human freedom at the instinctual and social levels. But there is more. The anarchistic release of men from the

[23] Sigmund Freud, "The Sexual Enlightenment of Children," *The Standard Edition IX,* 139.
[24] Herbert Marcuse, *Eros and Civilization,* 3ff. and 11ff.

control of repression and surplus-repression without a sweeping transformation of the present society and the performance principle by which it survives would lead not to freedom, but to the very opposite. Civilization itself would be overwhelmed in a burst of brutal and aggressive energy, which, for too long, has been accustomed to serving the interests of a brutal and aggressive society.

The question whether a "non-repressive sublimated" society is possible is from the very first a question of politics, of transforming the established society into one in which the need for domination and surplus-repression no longer exists. Beyond that, the degree to which repression itself can be eliminated is an open issue. For Freud, repression is the irreversible price of civilization; for Marcuse, men living under different social, political, and economic conditions might in turn create freer institutions under which the need for repression would be greatly diminished.

"Sex and politics" is more than a mere slogan. For the degree of control exercised over the population of advanced industrial societies is rooted in manipulation at the instinctual level on a scale impossible prior to the advent of the means and the products of industrialization. The prescription of channels for the expression of libidinous energy in directions which are politically useful to the ruling powers has also been enhanced by technology. The result is a population which is increasingly docile *and* aggressive, content in domination while hating and destroying the things one is supposed to hate and destroy. The masters emerge stronger than ever.

Non-repressive civilization can only be considered as the outcome of political changes which would re-program the computers from overkill and moonshots to the satisfaction of human needs and would abolish the performance principle under which most men toil for the benefit of a few.

The political break in the chain of control might, indeed, lead to a break in the chain of unequal, alienated toil and the establishment of a society of non-repressive, sublimated libidinal relationships in the place of the universal cash-nexus. But it is only a political transformation that offers the hope that the destruction of one historical form of the performance principle is not tantamount to the destruction of civilization.

Eros and Civilization raises the possibility of a society without surplus-repression; but the work is not a call for immediate or "unrestricted gratification" of the sexual instinct:

Freud did not define the "essence" of love as sexual desire, but as the inhibition and sublimation of sexual desire by tenderness and affection, and he saw in this "fusion" one of the greatest achievements of civilization. Consequently, Freud could not have had the idea" (and I did not) that "the emancipation" of man lies in the complete and unrestricted satisfaction of his sexual desire.[25]

At the same time, Marcuse agrees with Freud's scathing denunciation of the excessive repression imposed on human sexuality by the erstwhile codes and practices of Victorianism.[26] But emancipation from surplus-repression requires far more than the unhampered release of private desires and hostilities in private and public.

II

With *One-Dimensional Man* Marcuse moves from the possibilities for a non-repressive society to the analysis of the

[25] Herbert Marcuse, "A Reply to Erich Fromm," *Dissent* (Winter, 1956), 79.
[26] Herbert Marcuse, *Eros and Civilization,* 200–201 and *passim.*

factors in advanced industrial society which perpetuate un-freedom and repression. The work involves an examination of the important cultural changes which occurred during the period between the wars and led to new forms of repression and domination. This critique of prevailing trends leads Marcuse to conclude that the new-found freedoms of the decade are not the harbingers of the emancipation rendered possible by the available technological liberation from toil and scarcity, but, in many instances, the signs of a new and more effective control at the deepest levels of man's instinctual being. But even superficially, the events of the decade in the sphere of sexual behavior have, if anything, strengthened the illusion of freedom in other areas and, by that very token, have served the interests of control behind the backs of individuals through the coordination of con-trol at the economic, political, and social levels. Once again Marcuse insists that the authentic emancipation of the individual from his own superfluity of repression depends upon the elimination of institutions which serve as the agents of repression and demand the rigged release of sublimated and desublimated energy for their survival. The release of repressed energy within the confines of the estab-lished order is the return to barbarism and the end of civilization—the process of regression which Freud warned against.

What are the new forces of repression which operate through the socialization process in advanced technological society? In order to discover what these forces are and how they operate in the formation of the individual personality, it is necessary first to examine the sweeping changes which have taken place in the economic, political, and social spheres since Freud's day. These changes include, first, the emergence of organized competition on the national and supra-national scale; second, the growing concentration of control by total administration and co-ordination of technology, culture, and politics; third, self-perpetuating mass production and consumption stimulated by advertising and the creation of artificial needs; fourth, the growing invasion and negation of privacy—physical, mental, and emotional —by manipulation and indoctrination.

According to Marcuse, these tendencies have the most serious and far-reaching consequences for both the individual whose psyche is formed under the prevailing features and, conversely, for the society made up of such individuals. For example, the father and the patriarchal family, which were formerly the chief agents of socialization, have been increasingly replaced by direct socialization through the mass media, education, sport teams, peer groups. The earliest psychic conflicts and subsequent repression emerged in the long struggle with the father; with the decline in the role of the father, the ego is increasingly formed directly "from outside," before consciousness can be shaped as the individual and relatively independent force which mediates between the id and the superego, between one's *self* and *others*.[27]

These changes in the process and agents of socialization render the individual himself one-dimensional because the content of the ego is infused from outside by the vested interests of the society. Similarly, immediate identification with the goals and projects of that society is greatly enhanced, for the individual quickly learns to experience the needs of the social system as his own personally felt needs. He is the object, conscious and unconscious, of the ad-

[27] An important discussion of this problem prior to the publication of *One-Dimensional Man* occurs in a paper delivered by Marcuse in September, 1963, to the American Political Science Association. The paper was translated into German and published under the title, "Das Veralten der Psychoanalyse," in *Kultur und Gesellschaft II* (Frankfurt am Main: Suhrkamp, 1965). See esp. 87ff.

116

ministered creation and satisfaction of such needs. The victims of the established performance principle are less autonomous, less capable of distinguishing Self from Other, freedom from unfreedom. The weakening of the ego in advanced industrial society helps to account for the un-ending stream of prose and verbalization about "identity crises." But the weakening of the ego also helps to explain the formation of "masses" and the emergence of the authoritarian personality who seeks to supplant the emptiness with the introjection of external authority, opinion, and the soothing balm of the expert. What can one say of an alleged democracy when the *demos* consciously and intentionally relinquishes its sovereignty and power of ultimate arbitration to the military-industrial experts who "know more"?[28]

The shrinking of consciousness leads to the predominance of the emotions over consciousness and conscience. The behavior of individuals is less mediated than immediate; action flows from the desire to achieve instant gratification. But even the channels for gratification are administered by and through the control and management of free time, the "massification" of privacy.

But it would seem that the substitution of the impersonal goals and aims of society and its agents of socialization for the individual's own processes of selection is less effective as a source of gratification to the individual. The problem is twofold: first, identification with the external ego-ideal evokes anxiety, hostility in competition with others, the impossibility of satisfactorily living up to expectations which often transcend individual potentialities—a situation which prevails more often than not with the hero idols of advertising and entertainment. The frustration of competition and failure activates aggressive energy. Second,

[28] *Ibid.,* 94.

identification with the external ego-ideal means that the aggressive goals of the repressive society are easily accepted as one's own. In turn, the aggressive energy, once mobilized, is available for direct cathexis in the defense of the performance principle and its specific features of aggression at home and abroad, its wasteful ventures which satisfy no known human need. (As bigger and more expensive weapon systems replace last year's model it is increasingly possible to find earlier models in parks as playthings.) But the impersonal aims and objects which are the result of "massified socialization" seem not to provide adequate gratification. Increased frustration in such circumstances would lead to an "escalation of psychic aggression."[29]

In *One-Dimensional Man* Marcuse speaks of "repressive desublimation" or "institutionalized desublimation." In the face of the obvious changes in sexual mores and practices, the so-called Puritan or Victorian morality of earlier periods has essentially the same status today as the concept of free, private enterprise—a shibboleth which is reiterated daily. Both are largely mythological and have long ago ceased to function in any crucial way in determining the character of the society as a whole. Both the moral and the economic myth, however, are still effective as ideology and propaganda. The myth of unhampered free competition is apparently an important component of the illusion of freedom created in the socialization process in advanced industrial society. Similarly, the myth of the predominance of Puritan standards of sexual conduct is an important ideological ingredient in the commercialization of sex on and off Broadway and in the market place. The myth of a

[29] See Marcuse's discussion, "Aggressiveness in Advanced Industrial Society," *Negations* (Boston: Beacon, 1968), 264.

revolution against a tradition which has long been weak or hypocritical is undoubtedly profitable. (One need not take seriously the remark of the woman from the hinterlands who wished to see *The Boys in the Band* because she thought it was a Broadway musical.)

For Marcuse, repressive desublimation extends liberty while intensifying domination. Previous societies imposed authoritarian restrictions on sexual behavior. But prior to the advent of technology, some restrictions were necessary for the survival of civilization as long as scarcity and the struggle against nature demanded perpetual toil. Advanced industrial society, paradoxically, has increased its control over the individual by extending the boundaries of freedom in regard to sexual behavior through prescribed channels of institutionalized desublimation, the integration of sexuality into commerce and industry, advertising, and entertainment. At the same time, sexuality is carefully isolated from the broader erotic components which, in the Freudian theory, provide the basis for all civilized human relationships. Individuals who seem no longer capable of utilizing their own faculties in work and in leisure time find solace in the packaged and structured outlets provided by the billion-dollar entertainment business. Indeed, the sexual revolution itself is largely the brainchild of that industry for profit. The commercialization and externalization of sex has meant a further reduction in the available modes of erotic cathexis and the contraction of libido from erotic to mere sexual gratification without the sublimated bonds of friendship and tenderness which constituted the greatest victory of civilization against the aggressive impulses.

The diminishing of erotic expression and sublimated sexuality leads to the intensification of sexual energy, whose expression is immediate in the terms provided under the

119

performance principle.[30] The society offers institutionalized channels for the direct expression of limited, but intensified, sexual drives: the result is the strengthening of the control over the individuals by the protective and repressive society: "The organism is thus being preconditioned for the spontaneous acceptance of what is offered."[31] If the autonomy of the individual, for Freud, was embodied in the allegiance he was able to retain to the Pleasure Principle in spite of the sacrifices to the Reality Principle, then today the diminished opposition and tension between the two principles serves to strengthen the latter; the individual blithely accepts the system which permits him to satisfy, at least partially but in a direct manner, his diminished instinctual needs.

If the foregoing account of the mechanism and results of the socialization process in advanced industrial society is accurate, then a new problem arises in terms of the Freudian theory. According to Freud, the opportunity for the comparatively open and non-repressive expression of libido in sublimated forms would lead to gratification. The frustration and consequent need for aggression would be lowered as a result. But today, the facts seem to indicate that the opposite is happening: greater sexual leeway together with an *increase* in aggressive behavior.

Marcuse tries to account for this phenomenon with the argument that the institutionalization and externalization of the socialization process together with the institutionalization and control of desublimated behavior would mean, in fact, the release and gratification of fragmented, partial, and localized sexuality. By calling forth only one component of the general sexual impulse, the desublimation "would be

[30] Herbert Marcuse, *One-Dimensional Man* (Boston: Beacon, 1964), 73–74.
[31] *Ibid.,* 74.

120

compatible with the growth of unsublimated as well as sublimated forms of aggression."[32] Here too, as with sexuality, the passive acceptance and approval by large portions of the population of the national purpose, above all the practice of genocidal warfare, would indicate controlled desublimation or institutionalized desublimation in the realm of aggression. Sublimated forms of aggression also seem to be on the increase as, for example, verbal abuse and aggressive propaganda from the top usurp the place of rational discourse.

Marcuse's explanation can be amplified in terms of Freudian theory. Freud proposes that the life-serving forces which enhance civilization are "to a great extent obtained through the suppression of what are known as the *perverse* elements of sexual excitation."[33] One of the components of sexuality is aggression (sadism) which is normally repressed and sublimated.[34] But in a society which has instituted desublimated channels of libidinal expression in the interest of aggressive national goals, any number of "perverse" components of the sexual instinct might be expected to emerge in the expression of sex, sadism and aggression included:

Sadism would then correspond to an aggressive component of the sexual instinct which has become independent and exaggerated and has been brought to the fore by displacement.[35]

Where sadism occurs, masochism is customarily in attendance also. Evidence of both is plentiful among the young who abuse their bodies and those of others through destructive drugs, medication, and decibel count. Some re-

[32] *Ibid.*, 78.
[33] Sigmund Freud, " 'Civilized' Sexual Morality and Modern Nervous Illness," *the Standard Edition IX*, 189. See also *"Three Contributions to the Theory of Sex," The Basic Writings of Sigmund Freud*, 553–579.
[34] Sigmund Freud, *"Three Contributions,"* 569.
[35] *Ibid.*, 569.

121

cent examples may suffice. In a report on "Rock Style," Sara Davidson quotes one rock performer as saying, "I've come on stage lots of times, just from the music, and it's unbelievable."[36] Another member of a rock group exposed himself on stage. Still another "set fire to his guitar." Other perverse components of the sexual instincts also seem rampant, sadism and masochism especially. Leather, gold rings through the nose, sound so loud as to cause pain, and sexual sadism itself. "Most of the girls . . . are interested in getting into whipping. You know, you take off your belt and kind of tease them with it, and then you start doing it harder."[37]

There is no greater success in the commercialization of sex-as-entertainment than the Playboy Enterprises of Hugh Hefner. In a lengthy series of articles on "The Playboy Philosophy," Hefner relies on Ayn Rand's concept of aggressive selfishness and on the stock liberal wisdom to invent the "playboy," the classic description of which follows:

He can be a sharp-minded young business executive, a worker in the arts, a university professor, an architect or engineer. He can be many things providing he possesses a certain point of view. He must see life not as a vale of tears, but as a happy time; he must take joy in his work, without regarding it as the end and all of living; he must be an alert man. . . . a man who—without acquiring the stigma of the voluptuary or dilettante—can live life to the hilt.[38]

Life is a "happy time" and, like work, fun. At one and the same time, Hefner defends capitalism and the status quo, and attacks Puritanism and censorship. Almost anything goes, apparently, so long as it is American, anti-socialistic,

[36] Sara Davidson, "Rock Style: Defying the American Dream," *Harper's* (July, 1969), 60.

[37] *Ibid.*, 57.

[38] Hugh M. Hefner, "The Playboy Philosophy," issued as a series of four pamphlets (Chicago: December, 1962), Pamphlet I, 3.

and successful. Not a word is said about poverty, alienation of labor, wars, racial discrimination, aggression at home and abroad, waste, pollution, nuclear idiocy—and nothing is said about love, friendship, or the other civilizing affections. As the "philosophy" unfolds, it becomes clear that eroticism plays no role in the life of the playboy. Sex as fun and entertainment with all the commercial accoutrements of sex appear to exhaust the range of human desires and expression.[39]

One-dimensional man, the victim and adjunct of advanced industrial domination, is isolated from the very instinctual roots of his unconscious memory and being by the process of surplus-repression at work in the formation of the ego and the contents of consciousness, in the controlled satisfaction of needs, and in the added stimulation and toleration of heretofore forbidden modes of behavior. For Marcuse, the most frightening element of the new performance principle is the manipulation and control of the psyche itself at the conscious and unconscious levels, for here lie the socio-psychological origins of the "tough baby," the authoritarian personality of our times,[40] the playboy. It has been noted previously that the playboy ethos "is basically *anti-sexual*. Like the sports car, liquor and hi-fi, girls are just another *Playboy* accessory."[41] While the statement accurately attests to the routine commercialization of sex, the term *anti-sexuality* fails to capture the reductionism of eroticism to sex: One looks in vain for the slightest hint of eroticism in the playboy network of products. The impulses which, in their sublimated forms, Freud viewed as the essence of civilization—the affections which curtail aggres-

[39] See the brief sketch entitled "Tough Baby," in Theodor W. Adorno, *Minima Moralia* (Frankfurt am Main: Suhrkamp, 1951), 51–2.

[40] Herbert Marcuse, *One-Dimensional Man*, 74.

[41] Harvey Cox, in J. D. Brown, ed., *Sex in the 60's* (New York: Time-Life, 1968), 40.

sion and bind people into enduring relationships of friend-ship—have all been reduced to their purely sexual (desub-limated) components: Joy becomes fun; friends become chicks or tricks; gratification becomes instant release; and Eros yields its power to instant sexuality. And sex itself has been studied, dissected, measured, observed, computerized, analyzed, quantified, standardized, sanitized, and reduced to the techniques of copulation in a thousand different books, articles, plays, and research centers. Thomas Nagel notes, ". . . it is tempting to regard as sadistic an excessive preoccupation with sexual technique, which does not per-mit one to abandon the role of agent at any stage of the sexual act."[42]

Civilization has arrived, then, at a stage where the in-struments of toleration, flexibility, and emancipation from old taboos are at the same time the vehicles of a form of domination and repression which is, perhaps, even more debilitating than the earlier patriarchal model of socializa-tion and psychosexual development. The latter, while de-manding surplus-repression, left the individual free, albeit surreptitiously in many cases, to explore his own body and the bodies of others in freedom. Today the agents of so-ciety who prescribe "freedom" have greatly narrowed the space for psychic maneuvering and exploration. Constant panels, discussions, lectures on norms and techniques by the media and in the academies have successfully isolated and compartmentalized sexual performance with at least four novel consequences.

(1) Sexuality itself is viewed as a laboratory specimen. It is thereby reduced to a mundane aspect of human be-havior, like eating an omelet,[43] and the expansive, erotic

[42] Thomas Nagel, "Sexual Perversions," 14.
[43] *Ibid*. See Nagel's discussion of the decisive differences between hunger and sexual motivation, pp. 8–9.

dimensions of libido are eliminated. The fullest range of relationships which are truly human is correspondingly reduced. It is as if the mock-ups of jovial and festive social gatherings which permeate the world of advertising in the media had all but replaced such gatherings and co-operative endeavors in life itself. Community projects in the arts, where they exist at all, must be the work of committees rather than the spontaneous expression of individual needs and talents.

(2) The commercialization and scientific study of sexual performance—even to the measurement of the size of genitalia and kinetic and organic sensations during orgasm—and the increasing dissemination of such information may well tend to establish norms or standards of behavior which are far more ritualistic and repressive than the outlandish standards of perfection found in romantic love, and which are every bit as impossible of attainment. The thorough-going application of technology to every aspect of sexuality robs the imagination, the source and repository of political, social, and personal alternatives, and poses a threat to the ego more frightening than the threat of the father.

(3) The inevitable failure to match the standards set by the commercial sex idols and ideology leads to enormous profits for the cosmetic and other industries; and it also leads both to a variety of psychological malfunctions, such as frustration and increased aggressiveness, in the continual public and private competition with the idols who serve as ego-ideals, and at the same time to passive resignation and shame which leave the individual more susceptible to that which is offered.

(4) The imposition of scientific and commercial standards of "emancipated" performance deprive the individual of the main source of his own freedom, the Pleasure Principle. For here is the most subversive discovery in the

Freudian theory: sex and politics are decisively linked—not only at the conscious level and through the forms of socialization—but also in the unconscious which strives for freedom from repression. More bluntly, freedom becomes ideology and propaganda unless the individuals in a society are relatively free both in consciousness and politically to develop and explore the erotic impulses without the presupposed, externally imposed standards of either Puritan morality or scientific, institutionalized research. There is no freedom without individuals who have charted their own course between the persistent demands of the Pleasure Principle and the demands of civilization without sacrificing all to either Aphrodite or Artemis.

But is the foregoing analysis of freedom really so very different from the credo of the "playboy"? There appear to be decisive differences which can best be illuminated through the analysis of an example—the ambiguity of the popular slogan, "Do your own thing." In some ways the slogan seems to capture the ambiguities of the present, both the increased domination and the possibilities for emancipation from sexual negation and sexual reductionism. The slogan contains both the passive acceptance of intolerable or even barbaric behavior and the refusal to submit to standards which are intolerable and barbaric. If the slogan means literally that anyone at the present time is justified in acting out his own whims, then civilization is surely doomed for the very reasons expounded by Freud. Not even the permissive thinkers of the Enlightenment believed that "anything goes" or that "one man's opinion is as good as another's."[44] On the other hand, the slogan is subversive of existing tendencies toward massification of socialization. the public orgasm, sexual reductionism, and increasing domination through toleration and liberation. Doing one's *own* thing implies the existence of a self which is different from the others, a conscious subject which creates for itself the alternatives to the superimposed demands of the performance principle and is conscious of the available alternatives to the "objectification" of the psyche.

Here again sex and politics are connected. The effort to survive as a free subject against the enormous pressures exerted by the established society cannot be expected to succeed as an individual undertaking or by patchwork reform:

Here, the old conflict arises again: human freedom is not only a private affair—but it is nothing at all unless it is *also* a private affair.[45]

In the passages cited earlier, Freud himself seemed to be aware of the impossibility of piecemeal change for the lessening of human subjugation and repression without a change in the entire structure of human institutions. Changing the whole is political change, revolutionary change, the effort to substitute a less repressive performance principle for one which amalgamates and utilizes psychic energy for increasing domination, global mastery, waste of human and natural resources, and the perpetuation of violence at home and abroad.

In summation, too many critics of the sexual "revolution" seem to have missed the decisive point. Apart from the usual voices in the wilderness announcing the moral col-

[44] For example, Voltaire explicitly rejects the toleration of intolerance and the evils of church-dominated education. It is only in an age which believes that there are no historically verified elements which are quintessential to civilization itself that the rhetoric of the ACLU prevails as accepted ideology. For the present, to ask the question, "Do you prefer George Lincoln Rockwell or John F. Kennedy or Ché Guevara?" seems tantamount to asking, "Do you prefer Liederkrantz, Camembert, or Brie?" in spite of the fact that for the majority of Americans the answer to the first question is a foregone conclusion on the basis of conditioning by the media without regard to political content and projects.

[45] Herbert Marcuse, *Eros and Civilization*, 224–25.

lapse of America through copulation, there are an increasing number of voices raised against the behavioral emancipation on typical pragmatic grounds. The usual argument of late runs something like the following: "Uncontrolled promiscuity, nudity, and the escalating defiance of the standards of taste and propriety will unleash a backlash and lead to the institution of a new age of Puritan suppression." It is dubious whether anyone except the commercial moguls who profit from the commercialization of sex would be the poorer if some of the trash were to disappear. But the main problem with the pragmatic argument is its fundamental ahistoricity. It is highly unlikely that the restoration of Puritanical codes could succeed unless corresponding political changes occur which lead to a full-scale totalitarian society; for the present society is itself too dependent upon the release and controlled gratification of libidinous instincts.

To be sure the possibility of political regression remains as a constant alternative, given the repressive features of the established society; similarly, liberation from those repressive features remains as a constant threat to the established society. But the path to liberation depends upon the refusal to participate in the public orgasm which, in many ways, still resembles and fortifies the process which D. H. Lawrence called "cultural masturbation." The refusal to participate depends on an immanent critique of the forces at work in and behind the sexual revolution and, conversely, on the remembrance and re-collection of the civilizing potentialities of Eros. The voyeurism and exhibitionism of the theatre, the authoritarian tendencies in the recent productions and public displays by the Living Theatre,[46] and

[46] Robert Brustein discussed the Living Theatre in an article which appeared in the *New York Review of Books*, vol. 12, no. 3 (February 13, 1969), 30–1.

128

the anti-erotic stimulation of the new sexuality threaten to destroy the fragile victories of sublimated sexuality. Freud noted the essential sublimation of sexuality involved in art, in the concept of beauty. The concept of beauty is rooted in "the soil of sexual stimulation . . . The more remarkable, therefore, is the fact that the genitals, the sight of which provokes the greatest sexual excitement, can really never be considered 'beautiful'."[47] Eros, like art, fulfills its civilized and civilizing mission not through sex alone, but through the channels of sublimation: "Whatever fosters the growth of culture works at the same time against the threat of war."[48] In a review of the Hungarian film *The Round Up,* Penelope Gilliat writes:

"The Round Up" is often about terror, but the style holds it back from horror, even in a scene where a naked girl has to run up and down before an obscene likeness of an honor guard, with the two lines of soldiers lashing her. The sight suddenly made me realize—maybe along with other people—why it is that the sight of the unknown naked bodies careering around stages and screens at the moment can mysteriously make you feel frightened; to anyone who remembers the films and newsreels of the Second World War these strangers without clothes summon up the concentration camps.[49]

III

Two questions remain to be discussed here: What is the precise relationship in Marcuse's theory between "surplus-repression" and "repressive desublimation?" What are the alternatives to the repressive ethics of Puritanism and to the repressive sexual explosion?

[47] Sigmund Freud, *"Three Contributions,"* 568n.
[48] Sigmund Freud, "Why War?" in Ernst Jones, ed., *The Collected Papers V* (New York: Basic Books, 1959), p. 287.
[49] Penelope Gilliat, in *The New Yorker* (May 17, 1969), 127.

There is an important adjunct to the first question. What justifies Marcuse in assuming that the sexual behavior at present is not the result of a *decline* in the actual amount of repression at the individual level and a decline in its attendant phenomena, guilt and anxiety, rather than the maintenance and even increase in repression? Why not assume that the new permissiveness is the result of a freer and more humane society which can, by that very token, subsume under the rubric of *sublimated behavior* a greater variety of pluralism of sexual practices? Isn't a society which survives and thrives on sexual plurality less repressive than one which demands heterosexual, procreative, genital-ized conformity and punishes deviance with the pain of guilt and, often, prison?

Yes, of course. And a question in response: What if the emancipation not only poses no threat to the established powers, but enhances the survival of a social system which threatens to liquidate civilization and life itself? What price the public orgasm if the resulting network of cathexis lends support to a society which is increasingly inimical to the preservation of civilization as it has developed?

Marcuse's historical extension of the Freudian theory necessitates an historical definition of sublimation. The term becomes meaningless if the point of reference is only the existing society, regardless of the degree to which that society threatens life and civilization, limits and distorts the imagination, and destroys the expansive and life-giving functions of the erotic impulses. Sublimation refers to those deflections of instinctual energy which enhance life and preserve the gains of civilization. And on that account, it is the established society itself which stands condemned for its reliance on behavior which is the antithesis of the fragile historical victory against ignorance and cruelty. The im-mediate expression and gratification of impulses—demanded, bestowed, and rewarded—belongs not to the historical realm of civilized existence, but to the primal horde. Given the objective preconditions for the survival of civilization, the tendencies of the present denote regression and *desublimation* to the degree that they suppress the remembrance and the rational defense of alternatives at both the instinctual and political levels.

But why *repressive?* Isn't the direct expression and acting out of unconscious and conscious desires indication enough that repression is on the wane? For Marcuse, the answer is no, although the content of repression may today be radically altered due to the drastic changes in the agents and processes of socialization since Freud. The raw aggressive and sexual impulses may no longer be repressed to the same extent required under the conflicts in the patriarchal society. But the compartmentalization of sexuality in advanced industrial society means that the truly erotic components of sexuality have been eliminated and repressed because of the threat they pose to the performance principle of that society.[50]

The same holds true for aggression. Sublimation has assumed a major role in the battle against and appropriation of nature for human ends. But the evidence today points to the betrayal of and expulsion from consciousness of the historical projects which led to the mastery over nature: a growing indifference to the environment (are cities in any other industrialized sector of the globe more violent, dangerous, hideous, and uninhabitable than those here?); wanton destruction, waste, pollution replace the appropriation of nature; the indifference toward and lack of concern for one's friends, neighbors, lovers. The quick trick and the one-night stand do not bespeak the language of liberation

[50] See the thorough-going discussion of this threat in *Eros and Civilization,* esp. Chapters II and X.

131

from repression, but the language of redoubled repression. Gone are the hopes for alternatives to the performance principle, only to be replaced by a weary and aggressive resignation. It is as if the Pleasure Principle had relinquished the eternal battle with the demands of the Reality Principle; or as if the Pleasure Principle itself had been repressed, forgotten, curtailed, and narrowed in exchange for the new and partial modes of satisfaction: A stupendous sacrifice. If repression had, indeed, declined, then one might expect, according to Freud, a corresponding decline in mental illness and the growth of permanent human relationships grounded in libidinal cathexis rather than cash-nexus and the "legitimate" contractual bonds of the courts of law.

The second question—of alternatives to the repression of sexuality under Puritanism and the repression of Eros under the governing powers of the sexual explosion—is a question of political, social, and psychological revolution. But no revolution is involved in a society which freely permits the regressive behavior of the commercial orgy and its attendant escapism to Zen, mysticism, and astrology. "Running wild in the woods, dyeing [oneself] with woad, and living on hips and haws,"[51] constitutes neither the expression of authentic individuality in the state of nature (a regressive reversal of civilization the impossibility of which Rousseau noted) nor the advent of a new emancipation in the midst of a destructive society. The belief that mysticism and ritual magic, performed by day or night, in or out of clothing, are proof of social transformation is but the latest example of repressive desublimation at the ideological level. In Haiti voodoo serves as a mask and support for carefully calculated repression by the authoritarian regime.

[51] Bertrand Russell, "Mysticism and Logic," *Mysticism and Logic* (Garden City: Doubleday, 1957), 15.

In advanced industrial society the celebration of the public orgasm and the mystical proclamation of change by means of enrapturing trances may serve a purpose not so very different.

But what are the alternatives? If desublimated self-indulgence reinforces the stranglehold of the prevailing destructiveness, the return to previous codes of repressive conduct, even if such a reversal were possible, could only revive and intensify the detection and punishment of "illegitimate" sexual behavior by more efficient technological means. The spectre of Calvin with technology at hand summons up nightmares.

Authentic alternatives to sexual desublimation must emerge within and against that desublimation itself. The transformation from sex-as-performance to erotic sexuality is at once a personal and a political project. The forces which severed the pathways that placed libidinal impulses into the service of civilization are political forces. In turn, the personal dissatisfaction and illness which result from the organized control of gratification and the social and political restriction of pathways for the expression of sublimated sexuality into channels which make any difference demand a politics which destroys and replaces the old. Under different social conditions, the pathways which currently lead to desublimation and sexual disturbances "must in health be supposed to serve . . . other than sexual aims, the sublimation of sexuality."[52] For Freud, the paths are also passable in both directions; natural and social environment created from sublimated sexual cathexis would in turn serve the interests of personal stimulation and gratification without outside interference or surplus-repression.

The hope for the alternative rests with those—both young and old—who reject the established organization of

[52] Sigmund Freud, *"Three Contributions,"* 603.

their personal lives and the expropriation of their physical and psychic energy for destructive ends. If the outcome of the struggle cannot be foretold, the ambiguities of the present trends should nonetheless be exposed; for in those ambiguities lies the cause of hope and despair.

First, together with the commercial proclamation of the sexual revolution, is the unannounced effort, especially among the students, to establish bonds of friendships which are not based upon the prevailing drive for profit. The greater toleration and flexibility offered by the society can be appropriated for ends, personal and political, which are fundamentally opposed to the social goals of the sexy commercial display. The opposition to those goals may destroy the repressive link between sexuality and the destructive performance principle.

Second, together with the repressive scientific reduction of sexuality to charts, graphs, and techniques comes the growing consciousness and possibility of making rational distinctions between impulses which are life-serving (erotic) and those which are destructive and aggressive. The choice among alternatives, the rational control which Freud defended over the destructive impulses, depends upon knowledge. To be sure, the new knowledge is both restricting and liberating—scientific control over the fundamental source of human freedom and creativity, on the one hand; and the defiance of that control through rational distinction and personal choice, on the other hand.

Nowhere is this ambiguity more evident than in the realm of the sexual perversions. Marcuse has amply demonstrated in *Eros and Civilization* that the weakest assumption in the Freudian theory was the unexamined link between the socially prescribed limitation of sexuality to genital-procreative sex and the productive and reproductive apparatus of the capitalist societies under the performance

134

principle of profitability. The extension of the erotic impulses to other zones of the body and to other forms of sexual behavior may threaten the established society at its most vital point because such non-productive sexuality threatens the productive apparatus which thrives on repressive sublimation and desublimation.[53] While the established society grows wealthy from the commercial exploitation of the perversions it creates, encourages, and tolerates, the perversions themselves retain their potential for disrupting the established performance principle. Here too distinctions are necessary and possible on a more rational basis than before, in the rejection by the individual himself of those "components" of sexuality that are destructive and partial, which distort or destroy the full erotic gratification and creation of which the individual is capable. Perversion itself would then require redefinition as "the truncated or incomplete versions of the complete configuration . . . perversions of the central impulse."[54] Narcissism, fetishism, sadism, masochism, under this redefinition, remain perverse. They are incomplete expressions of the demands of Eros. And so it is with sexual reductionism. The civilizing mission of Eros is defeated when the orgasm replaces the Pleasure Principle as the sole end of human sexuality:

> If sex were all, then every trembling hand
> Could make us squeak, like dolls, the wished-for words.
> But note the unconscionable treachery of fate,
> That makes us weep, laugh, grunt and groan, and shout
> Doleful heroics, pinching gestures forth
> From madness or delight, without regard
> To that first, foremost law . . .[55]

---

[53] Herbert Marcuse, *Eros and Civilization,* 44ff. and 161ff.
[54] Thomas Nagel, "Sexual Perversions," 13.
[55] From Wallace Stevens, "Le Monocle de Mon Oncle," *The Collected Poems* (New York: Knopf, 1954).

One-Dimensionality: The Universal Semiotic
of Technological Experience

JEREMY J. SHAPIRO

If only that which is true (the Logos; the Idea) really *is,* then
the reality of immediate experience partakes of the μὴ ὄν, of that
which is *not.* And yet, this μὴ ὄν, *is,* and for the immediate experience (which is the unique reality for the vast majority of
men) it is the only reality which *is.*

Herbert Marcuse, *One-Dimensional Man*

The present essay was written against the background of
two events significant for the radical movement in the
United States: the landing of men on the moon and the
process of disintegration of left-wing politics initiated by
the Chicago SDS convention in July, 1969.[1] The former
is a manifestation of a society whose technological rationality has completely transmuted terrestrial, human, and now
cosmic reality: the society Herbert Marcuse has called
"one-dimensional" and whose essential features, those

[1] This essay is a condensation, undertaken specially for this volume,
of part of a larger work in progress. Because the author has translated works of Herbert Marcuse, he wishes to note that Professor
Marcuse has not seen or discussed with him any of this essay and
is not responsible for any of the views expressed herein.

which distinguish it from the social structure depicted by orthodox Marxian theory, he has described and analyzed. The latter represents a failure of nerve. It is world-historically absurd that a political movement claiming to be the vanguard of the interests of humanity in view of its historical possibilities should be flagellating itself to death with the whip of mythology and infantilism at the moment after which every person born will no longer be a terrestrial animal. The original impetus of the current radical movement, as Paul Breines writes in his essay, was the experience of one-dimensional society, and the attempt to formulate this experience and turn it into a source of radical social change motivated its theory and practice. But the widening gap that separates the movement from historical trends points to contradictions and inadequacies in both experience and its formulation.

The movement's absurdity is no accident: as in the development of individual neurosis, so in history, situations of anxiety, in this case the catastrophe of liberation, provoke regression and the repetition compulsion. The gap between experience and the framework in which it is approached provokes desperate, self-destructive attempts to shore up the framework. Only the re-examination of experience, the attempt to integrate past and present, fantasy and reality, can help. That is why my primary purpose in the present essay is to restate Marcuse's theory of one-dimensionality and to make it more concrete, largely by bringing it into relation to the contributions of other thinkers. I shall argue that one-dimensionality operates as a universal semiotic of technological experience in which all of the oppositions of two-dimensional civilization are irreversibly homogenized and subjected to self-regulating laws of a synchronic system in which the traditional distinctions of form and matter, subject and object, the conscious and

137

the unconscious, and the beautiful and the necessary are overcome. This universal semiotic is the ground of all future political and social development. I shall then briefly suggest the appropriate way of dealing with one-dimensionality.[2]

In order to explain the character and genesis of one-dimensionality it is necessary to distinguish between three historical periods corresponding to three prevailing types of social organization: traditional pre-industrial society organized around direct political authority expressed as a relation between status groups, capitalist industrial society organized around political authority mediated through exchange relations, and advanced capitalist industrial society organized around political authority mediated through technology and relations of purposive rationality (because of the change in the function of exchange in the last type it bears great similarity to socialist industrial society). That these ideal types overlap in history makes their analysis difficult. Indeed the second type is not a pure type but merely a mode of transition between the first and the third. These types are correlated with specific forms of political and social organization as well as with forms of experience and modes of existence, such as mental and manual labor, freedom and necessity, art and utility, consciousness and the unconscious, and the individual and society.

Pre-industrial, traditional societies were stratified on the basis of status, and domination took the form of the political domination of lower by higher status groups.[3] Con-

---

[2] In all of the following I am indebted to the work not only of Marcuse but also of Jürgen Habermas, Henri Lefebvre, the French structuralist school (particularly Roland Barthes), Lewis Mumford, the modern design movement, Gilbert Simondon, and Tom Nairn, all of whom have been concerned with the nature and problems of one-dimensional man.

[3] I am using the expression "status groups" not in the limited sense of groups differentiated according to honor, in Weber's sense, but in that of groups differentiated on a wider basis than that of market

trol of the means of production and the exploitation of physical labor were part of this system of domination. In comparison to industrial society, the production process utilized a small amount of physical plant, machinery, and science, so that physical labor was the predominant factor of production. This gave rise to two aspects of the relationship between mental and manual labor. It is important to note that there is no such thing as "purely" manual or mental labor. All manual labor involves thought, co-ordination, planning, habitual knowledge, and all mental labor involves some action, operations, behavior. In pre-industrial society the relation of mental and manual labor took two specific forms: (1) their unity in the work of the craftsman or artisan; and (2) the separation of the latter as utilitarian, economic, and inferior labor (given "manual" status) from the political, regulating, "cultural" labor (given "mental" status) of the upper status groups. The effect of capitalism was to separate the mental and manual aspects of economic labor and integrate them through the functional unity of the machine process, while integrating the "separate" mental labor of the upper status groups into the utilitarian realm by means of the market mechanism and the bureaucratic hierarchy.[4]

Status stratification in pre-industrial society had its particular forms of social and political conflict and change, whose primary characteristic was the direct confrontation of status groups, made possible by the political form of domination. An institutional example of this was the Estates General, and modern parliaments are its offshoots.

---

position, income, or ownership of means of production, that is, including honor, legal rights and obligations, civil and political status, and so forth.

[4] This subject and its significance in the evolution of Marxian theory are treated in detail in my unpublished paper, "Mental and Material Labor: A Study of Marxism."

The interactional, political character of the relation of status groups made possible specific forms of the adaptation of the upper groups to the lower in situations of conflict—for example, the granting of specific rights—and also had particular forms of rigidity, that is, refusal or inability to adapt due to status-bound means (for example, honor) of conceiving of interests. The great modern revolutions were revolutions by estates: the bourgeois revolutions and peasant revolutions. With the dissolution of direct political domination and its replacement by a market society and the consequent predominance of class over status relations, revolution in the classical sense became impossible. Classes cannot make revolutions because they are economic, not political strata.[5]

It was the relatively low level of technical development in pre-industrial society that created the division of the world into two dimensions in the labor process, in experience, and in thought. In the pre-technical period, man confronts the objective world as form confronts matter. The

form-intention is not part of the matter on which labor is expended; it expresses a utility or a necessity for man, but it does not arise from nature. The activity of labor is what makes the bond between natural matter and form, which is of human provenance; work is an activity that succeeds in making two realities as heterogeneous as matter and form coincide, in rendering them synergic. And the activity of labor makes man conscious of the two terms that he synthetically places in relation.[6]

This relation is at the root of the series of dualisms that are

[5] This is what Lenin was referring to in writing that "social-democracy represents the working class, not in its relation to a given group of employers, but in its relation to all classes in modern society, to the state as an organized political force." *What is to be Done?* (New York: International Publishers, 1943), 56.

[6] Gilbert Simondon, *Du Mode d'Existence des Objets Techniques* (Paris: Aubier-Montaigne, 1958), 242.

characteristic of Western civilization: form and matter, universal and particular, man and nature, mind and body, labor and leisure, and the conscious and the unconscious. The entire experience of man is captured and organized in this series of dualisms, which are all structured vertically, the higher against the lower. And the quality of this relation was the *irreducibility* of the lower to the higher. It was the awareness of this dichotomy, the *déchirement ontologique* or *chorismos,* that motivated philosophical attempts to construct their unity, a system of reason in which the particular, the irrational, the thing-in-itself could be shown to be subject to and derived from the universal, the rational, the form. All such attempts foundered since they took place in the realm of forms (thought) itself and not in the real relation between form and matter. For, owing to the incomplete technical mastery of the world in the social labor process, "pre-technical knowledge is also pre-logical, in the sense that it constitutes a coupling of terms without discovering the interiority of the relation . . ."[7]

The inability to grasp the individual within the forms of reason led to the devaluation of the senses and their perceptions as sources of knowledge, since they transmit those aspects of reality that have not been subjected to the forms of reason and control; they transmit "secondary," not "primary" qualities. They communicate the "accidental," that which does not have the quality of necessity. Here is the root of the separation of the realms of the beautiful and useful, of art and industry. For in art, the universal and the particular, form and matter, are perfectly mediated. Here the "interiority of the relation" is present and constructed—but on a level different, and therefore less true, than that on which man confronts the world for the sake of self-preservation, where the interiority of the

7 *Ibid.,* 244.

relation has not yet been discovered. As we shall see below, it is the perfection of technology that makes possible the mediation of art and industry and the integration of the language of information with that of the senses.

Capitalism destroyed in two ways the social order whose features I have just sketched: through the quantification and generalization of exchange relations and through technology. Although both of these were essential to capitalism, the characteristic development of the past two centuries has been determined by their temporal order: in the first phase, exchange was the more important factor; in the second, technology gained priority. What the two have in common is purposive rationality. Both of them are vehicles for the translation of relations of political domination, based on symbolic interaction, into relations of instrumental action.[8] Through them, political domination could develop in the direction of a self-regulating system: political content becomes invisible in fetishism. Exchange generates commodity fetishism, and technology generates the fetishism of science and technology, or, as we shall see below, the fetishism of images and the technical object.

The impact of capitalism was to translate an entire sphere of political and status relations into exchange relations.

Only with the capitalist mode of production can the legitimation of the institutional framework be immediately linked with the system of social labor. Only now can the property order change from a *political relation* to a *production relation,* because it

[8] The distinction between work (instrumental and strategic action) and (symbolic) interaction and the parallel distinction between *techne* and *praxis* have been elaborated as central concepts of sociological theory by Jürgen Habermas, especially in *Technik und Wissenschaft als 'Ideologie'* and *Erkenntnis und Interesse,* both published in Frankfurt am Main by Suhrkamp Verlag in 1968 and to be published in English translation by Beacon Press. The present essay is indebted to Habermas' work in a way that cannot be indicated adequately by means of individual references.

legitimates itself through the rationality of the market, the ideology of exchange society, and no longer through a legitimate order of domination. It is now the system of domination that can be justified on the basis of the legitimate relations of production. . . . The institutional framework of society is only mediately political and immediately economic (the bourgeois constitutional state as "superstructure").[9]

As reciprocity and interaction, the exchange of services, functions, and objects is a primary structure in all societies. Such exchange may be a relation of domination by means of authority, status, control, including the control of resources, tools, and labor, and disparity in decision and communication with attendant suppression and distortion of human needs. In pre-capitalist societies, where such exchange relations are not quantifiable and cannot receive mathematical expression, the extent of equality and the criterion of domination are qualitative as well as quantitative, and differences of wealth appear mixed with differences of status and authority. Under capitalism exchange takes on a quantitative form. In commercial capitalism, the principle of equality in value becomes the basis of exchange and the precondition of its extension, while the possibility of profit derives from monopoly or control which is not itself present in the act of exchange. Thus the economic relation of quantitative equality between exchange partners takes place within a political relation of qualitative inequality.

In industrial capitalism the principle of quantitative exchange is extended from the relation between exchangers of commodities to the relation between exchanger and producer. One aspect of the political relation between the two, namely, monopoly and control of the means of production by the exchangers of commodities (capitalists) as

[9] Habermas, *Technik und Wissenschaft,* 70.

143

a class, makes possible both the quantification of the reciprocal relation between capitalists and producers (workers) through the labor contract, and a specific form of quantitative inequality: namely, the cession by the capitalist to the worker of a smaller quantity of commodities (as wages, that is, purchasing power over commodities) than that ceded by the worker to the capitalist. Now in any society that invests, purchasing power will be less than the value of the total commodities produced. Under capitalism, however, this inequality takes the form of inequalities of income between classes, based on inequalities of control and decision, which are themselves not peculiar to capitalism. But the extension of exchange makes possible the comparison of the quantified aspect of the relation between capitalists and workers with the quantified aspect of the relation between capitalists. That is, a bourgeois standard derived from commerce can be applied to the relations of production.[10]

This comparison was the basis of Marx's economic theory, especially the theory of surplus value. His error was both to define capitalist production in terms of this aspect of the political relation between capitalists and workers and to explain the political relation in terms of this aspect. This error was compounded by a false perception of contemporary social change. Because the initial stages of capitalist industrialization were accompanied by a rapid expansion of the labor market and the creation of a large and impoverished proletariat drawn from the peasantry and artisans, while science had still not been extensively applied to industry, it became possible to confuse

[10] That is, exchange equivalence is the principle of legitimacy according to which the exchange of labor power is adjudged illegitimate. This is why, in Habermas' words, *"The critique of political economy was, according to Marx, the theory of bourgeois society only as critique of ideology." Ibid.,* 76.

144

characteristics of the class relations and conflicts of the economic system with the status relations and conflicts persisting from the previous social order. In reality, "The primacy of politics over economics was always a fact,"[11] and Marx recognized this at various points. But the dissolution of earlier modes of social organization made it seem as though economics had replaced politics. Thus the anti-capitalist manifestations provoked by the new system, whose high point was the role of artisans and the urban lower classes in the revolution of 1848, were interpreted by Marx as attributes of the working class in the economic system of capitalism, when in fact they were the result of the effect of capitalism within the previously existing political and social system.[12] Marx, however, used these political conflicts as a rationale for applying the model of traditional status conflicts and of bourgeois revolutions to the internal dynamic of capitalism itself.

The labor theory of value and its corollary, the theory of surplus value, were adopted by Marx at the very point when capitalism was making them obsolete. He did so in order to guarantee the congruence of the new economic system and the traditional political system, to achieve a strict parallel between the political relation of the lower social group to the higher, and the economic relation of this group to the rest of society. The movement of the self-regulating economic system would coincide with the development of political conflict between the working class and the bourgeoisie: the latter conflict would necessarily follow from the former. To do this Marx was forced to deny the reality of exchange and its inherent political character, for

[11] Franz Neumann, "Economics and Politics in the Twentieth Century," in Herbert Marcuse, ed., *The Democratic and the Authoritarian State* (Glencoe: Free Press, 1957), 268.

[12] See Theodore Hamerow, *Restoration, Revolution, Reaction* (Princeton: Princeton University Press, 1958).

his theory compelled him to assert that the salaried manual labor of the working class is exchanged against *nothing* and to interpret all aspects of the functional social division of labor as transformations of this abstract labor. At an early stage of capitalism, the expansion of the labor market and the relative lack of incorporation into the system of science and control as productive forces combined with the needs of ideology gave the labor theory of value an apparent plausibility. But, as Marx himself noted, it is "modern industry which makes science a productive force distinct from labor,"[13] and this, along with other developments, made Marx's theory obsolete by the end of the 19th century. Not only did scientific technology begin to displace the proletariat as the primary productive force, but the technification of direction and control through the bureaucratization of enterprises as well as the intervention of the state into the economy and the introduction of capitalist planning represented new forms of the self-regulation of capitalism as a political system. Thus the seeming coincidence of the status relations of pre-capitalist society with the class relations of the economic system was dissolved. As a closed, self-regulating system the capitalist *economy* could not lead in any case to revolutionary political conflict, since it operates on the basis of the subjection of all to the laws of the system (this insight was the basis of Leninism). But the new forms of political domination made the pre-capitalist form of *political* conflict (of which Leninism is an example) obsolete as well. Thus the transformation of capitalism dried up the sources of proletarian revolution. Exchange became a form of domination not so much as a source of extraction of surplus labor, but as a form of self-regulation *per se,* that is, as a form of reification.

[13] *Capital, The Communist Manifesto, and Other Writings,* Max Eastman, ed. (New York: Random House, 1932), 86.

The critique of exchange expressed in the Marxian theory of exchange value also derives from a transitional state of affairs. The notion of exchange value was radical against the background of the pre-capitalist tradition of production for use. In the words of Henri Lefebvre, the

> reference to productive activities, to the 'values' of creation that were inseparable from production . . . [associated] fact and value. ˙. . . In this sense, *Kapital* (1867) brought to theoretical language a philosophical 'consensus' that was only slightly conscious outside of that misunderstood work, which misunderstood its own conditions.[14]

With the eradication of the tradition of production for use, there is no value with which exchange value can be compared, and the concept ceases to be critical *per se*. All strata can thus be integrated into the system by means of consumption as a mode of life. When the expansion of capitalism led to an extension from the bourgeoisie to the working class of consumption and its augmentation, the latter's needs were defined by the purely internal dynamic of the economy. Marx thought of the proletariat as a revolutionary class because it had needs that could not be met by capitalism.[15] And as Freud wrote, the hostility of the masses to civilization derives from their resentment at the instinctual renunciation imposed upon them "by a culture whose existence they make possible by their work, but in whose wealth they have too small a share."[16] The expansion of consumption makes possible the satisfaction of

[14] *La Vie Quotidienne dans le Monde Moderne* (Paris: Gallimard, 1968), 212. This book, which is full of crucial insights into one-dimensional society, some of them derived from structuralism, is in places rambling and confused to the point of incoherence. A *précis* of it would be valuable for English readers.

[15] Herbert Marcuse, Preface to Raya Dunayevskaya, *Marxism and Freedom* (New York: Bookman, 1958), 12.

[16] *The Future of an Illusion* (New York: Doubleday, 1964), 15.

147

these needs to the point where they no longer threaten the social order.

"The example of the automobile may serve as an illustration. . . . If the automobile (or other machine) is libidinally cathected over and above its use value as vehicle . . . it clearly provides substitute gratification."[17] Things come alive, objects become magical. Through the exchange process objects are transformed into signs and signs into objects.[18] Through the absorption of use value into exchange value, uses become only meanings. In the words of Roland Barthes,

Every use is converted into a sign of this use. . . . As our society produces only standardized, normalized objects, the objects are fated to be the executions of a model, the speech-acts of a language, the substances of a signifying form. . . . This universal semantization of use is capital: it translates the fact that there is nothing real that is not intelligible.[19]

Through this process, in which objects and signs are homogenized, exchange becomes the exchange of meanings.[20] Consumption becomes the consumption of signs as well as of objects, and objects in any case obtain their qualities from their meanings.[21] In this way, the process of produc-

[17] Herbert Marcuse, "The Obsolescence of the Freudian Concept of Man," in *Five Lectures,* translations by Jeremy J. Shapiro and Shierry M. Weber (Boston: Beacon, 1970).

[18] Lefebvre, 214. See also Claude Lévi-Strauss on the promotion of an object to the status of sign, quoted in Yvan Simonis, *Claude Lévi-Strauss ou la "Passion de l'Inceste"* (Paris: Aubier-Montaigne, 1968), 102f.

[19] Roland Barthes, *Éléments de Sémiologie* (Paris: Editions Gonthier, 1965), 114.

[20] Marx referred to this in the 1844 manuscripts in describing money as "the means and capacity of transforming the idea into reality and reality into a mere idea." "Nationalökonomie und Philosophie," *Die Frühschriften,* Siegfried Landshut, ed. (Stuttgart: Kroner, 1964), 300.

[21] Lefebvre, 195 and 205f.

tion and consumption is converted into a semiotic system, in which

the totality of significations naturally forms a system based on distinctions and oppositions, since these significations are relative to one another, and a synchronic system, since these relations are interdependent.[22]

Below we shall see how this result of the universalization of exchange brought about, in combination with the neotechnic revolution, the collapse of referentials and laid the foundations for the universal semiotic of technological experience.

Another significant effect of exchange relations was individualization, that is, the reduction of social relations to patterns of individual exchange acts. In early Western civilization, beginning with the Greek city, the individual emerged out of a conflict between social institutions, originally the family and the city. Being embedded in conflicting institutions with defined limits and taboos made it possible for the individual to define himself or be defined. The "taboo horizons" of these social groups, that is, the distinction between in-group and out-group with regard to incest and aggression, created a natural-social order which limited the individual while at the same time giving him a relatively closed institutional background *against* which he could assert and develop his individuality.

These horizons also classified types of human relations: community (*Gemeinschaft*) versus society (*Gesellschaft*), affective versus affectively neutral, exogamy and incest, friends and enemies. These differences unambiguously defined transgression and distinguished legitimate from illegitimate guilt. The exchange relation broke down these boundaries. The weakening of the role of the family as the

---

[22] Jean Piaget, *Le Structuralisme* (Paris: P.U.F., 1968), 65.

institutional framework of individuality and as the definition of taboo horizons, the reduction of social relations to
exchange acts, and the interpenetration of communal
(*Vergemeinschaftung*) and associative relationships (*Ver-
gesellschaftung*) have resulted not only in the loss of in-
ternalization and inner-directedness but in the *spreading* of
incest, aggression, and transgression through the entire
system of social relations. Freud described this process in
individual psychology in talking of the communicability of
taboo as an electric charge that may spread out in all directions to all objects and thoughts.[23] The extension of taboo
in the exchange system attenuates it in its prior sphere so
that it becomes a quality of objects, signs, persons, and
relations, rather than a force that prohibits them, while
being extended to spheres previously beyond taboo. This
is how life can become a perpetual Saturnalia, a lived
moving picture. For incest and aggression enter into all
human relations instead of being kept in place by rigid
taboo horizons. And they can charge the most apparently
neutral and trivial forms of human relations. The system
sustains itself through the most minute social interactions,
and advanced industrial society turns into a vast network
of people who are engaged in manipulating and repressing
each other. "The most widely and immediately relevant
meaning-schemes [become] those of primary group relationships."[24]

It is in this context that we must understand the genesis
both of modern neurosis and of psychoanalysis. Inadequate
as Freud's conception of the nature of philosophy, religion,
and culture was, his discussion of their relation to neurosis
is suggestive. According to Freud's formulation in *Totem*

[23] *Totem und Tabu* (Frankfurt am Main: Fischer, 1956), 27ff.
[24] Herbert Fingarette, *The Self in Transformation* (New York:
Harper, 1965), 59.

and Taboo, neurosis is caused in large part by the reduction of the *social* component of relations with others, that is, concern for them, in favor of the sexual component.[25] Then, speaking of neuroses as distortions of art, religion, and philosophy, he writes that in the last analysis the reason for this distortion is that the neuroses are asocial formations and

attempt to achieve with private means what in society originated through collective labor. In the instinct analysis of the neuroses one finds that in them instinctual forces of sexual origin exercise the determining influence, while the corresponding cultural forms are based on social instincts, which have arisen out of the unification of egoistic and erotic components . . . [The] real world avoided by the neurotic is ruled by the society of men and the institutions they have created together: turning away from reality is simultaneously a secession from the human community.[26]

Translating this into the present frame of reference, we can say that the exchange relation, by eliminating the sphere of communal socio-cultural institutions or reducing their content to what can be comprised in individual acts of exchange, eliminates the social (in Freud's sense) component of social relations, their quality of sharing in trans-instrumental purposes, their "collective labor," which was also the basis of their sublimated aspect. "Sexual gratification is above all the private affair of the individual,"[27] and the privatization inherent in capitalist exchange relations transforms them into relations overcharged with sexual content. In such relations man confronts man in "secession from the human community." This is the basis of what Marcuse has called repressive desublimation. Furthermore,

25 Page 84.
26 *Ibid.*
27 *Ibid.,* 85.

the transformation of common cultural meanings into neuroses is the pre-condition of psychoanalysis. For the dissolution of the transindividual, more-than-primary-group legitimation of these meanings is the disenchantment that makes possible their comprehension as individual constructions. The cultural world comes to exist only as my world.

Under the impact of science and technology, the political character of the exchange relation was transformed. It served the function of domination by relating men to each other as things and as means, by removing social processes operating through the exchange relation from the sphere of decision, control, and subjectivity, and by creating a network through which patterns of domination could be spread throughout society, a system of self-regulating signs, objects, and individuals. But it still operated with traditional means and units, people, and commodities, within the framework of two-dimensional civilization. The neotechnic phase of technological development, which began in the second half of the 19th century and became predominant around 1910, took over the exchange system and used it for its own ends. By reshaping the human, mechanical, and natural worlds, breaking them down into their basic units and principles of relation, it transformed the system of exchange into the universal semiotic of technological experience: one-dimensionality as a system of political domination through technology.

According to Patrick Geddes, who invented the term, and Lewis Mumford, "the neotechnic phase represents a third definite development of the machine during the last thousand years."[28] At the same time it is an historical unit with characteristic patterns of social organization, typical

[28] Lewis Mumford, *Technics and Civilization* (New York: Harcourt, Brace, and World, 1963), 212.

materials, sources of energy and forms of power, means of communication, culture, and art. Its technical base was initiated around the middle of the 19th century with the invention of the electric cell, the storage cell, the dynamo, the motor, the electric lamp, and the spectroscope, the perfection of the water-turbine, and the discovery of the conservation of energy. It began to impinge upon the paleotechnic phase (the Industrial Revolution) between 1875 and 1900, when these inventions were applied to industrial processes, most notably in electric power stations and electronic means of communication (telephone and telegraph). Alloys, rare earths, light metals, and synthetic compounds began to supplant iron, wood, and glass. Most important, science was directly applied to technics and to the conduct of life; it adapted mechanism to biology and physiology, was institutionalized as part of the industrial process, and displaced the proletariat as the mainstay of production. Finally, out of this arose a new synthesis of art and technology, of man and nature, which destroyed two-dimensional civilization by consummating the centuries-long process of technological mediation.

Two-dimensional civilization was based, as we saw above, on the external quality of the confrontation of man and nature, form and matter, and on the corresponding irreducibility of the lower level to the higher, of the individual to the universal. The individual, in its materiality, is the limit of the project of rationality as a system of laws and relations, since the individual cannot be deduced and subjected to operations as laws and relations can. What broke down two-dimensional into one-dimensional civilization was the process of technological mediation, in which the world is transformed operationally so that subject and object, form and matter, are mediated through action, operation, and function:

153

Functioning is operation and operation is functioning. One cannot speak of the work of a machine but only of its function, which is an ordered totality of operations. Form and content, if they still exist, are on the same level, are part of the same system; there is continuity between technology and nature.[29]

Where the two-dimensional world was characterized by conflicts between antitheses, technology brings about "the convergence of functions in a structural unity rather than a compromise between conflicting exigencies."[30] At the same time the machine, as mediator between man and nature, creates continuity not only between technology and nature but also between technology and man, whose structure is assimilated to that of machines and technologically shaped natural objects:

One may call pure information that which has not the character of an event, that which can only be comprehended if the subject that receives it gives rise in himself to a form analogous to the forms borne by the supplier of information (the technical object). . . . For a technical object to be received as technical and not merely useful, for it to be judged as the result of invention, as a bearer of information and not as a utensil, the subject that receives it must possess technical forms within himself.[31]

This reciprocal adaptation of man, machine, and nature, in which things and individuals are dissolved into relations and functions, takes place in the field of action:

Mathematical propositions thus express "a general accommodation to the object." [But] mathematical entities are not therefore the result of an abstraction based on objects but rather of an abstraction made in the midst of "actions as such." Logico-mathe-

29 Simondon, 244.
30 *Ibid.,* 22.
31 *Ibid.,* 247f.

154

matical abstraction . . . is, as pure co-ordination, the general form of action—"action as such."[32]

The genesis of this new form of functional, structural unity, eliminates the hierarchical, vertical relations of the two-dimensional world, transposing them into a single, horizontal level. In doing so, and in reducing individuality to universality, it makes possible the extension of the field of operation of the system of reason to what previously existed as matter and the individual. Thus a self-regulating system is established; nothing is outside it, because technology has already created the mediations or schematism through which whatever is outside can be integrated without the crossing of barriers. Such a system is the "structure" of the structuralists:

a system of transformations, which as a system comprehends laws (in contrast to the properties of the elements) and which conserves itself or enriches itself through the mere play of its transformations without the latter going beyond the frontiers of the system or having recourse to external elements. In a word, a structure thus includes the three characteristics of totality, transformations, and self-regulation.[33]

It is clear that the distinction here between laws and elements is analytical, and that the elements themselves cannot be outside the structure. Otherwise the system could not enrich itself; its ability to do so derives exclusively from the technological mediation between form and content.

The notion of information as the link between man and machine points to the general process of semiotization as the basis for this system. Above we saw the root of this in the extension of exchange. Technological mediation in-

---

[32] Herbert Marcuse, *One-Dimensional Man* (Boston: Beacon, 1964), 160f. Internal quotations from Jean Piaget, *Introduction a l'épistémologie génétique* (Paris: P.U.F., 1950), 3:287ff.

[33] Piaget, *Le Structuralisme,* 6f.

tensifies it and gives it new aspects. For technological thought is based on communication and participation. That is why

above the social community of labor and beyond the interindividual relation that is not supported by an operatory activity, a mental and practical universe of technicity establishes itself, in which human beings communicate through that which they invent. The technical object taken in accordance with its essence, that is to say the technical object insofar as it has been invented, thought, willed, and assumed by a human subject, becomes the support and the symbol of that relation which we should like to name *transindividual*.[34]

The technical object is communication *per se,* and the world of technical objects becomes the medium of intersubjectivity.

Thus the technological mediation between the two dimensions takes place in the medium of a semiotic system of communication: communication between men and between man, machine, and nature. The extension of technological rationality leads to a formalization of communication in the realms of technology, labor, and interpersonal relations, which we have seen heralded in the exchange system. Now both language and functional sign and symbol systems become integrated into a larger system. Below we shall see in more detail how modern design becomes the form of this system and absorbs all the objects and details of daily life. What is important here is to observe that the process of semiotization led to the "collapse of referentials."[35] The elimination of two-dimensional civilization and of values transcending the exchange process, the transformation of objects into signs, the rise of manufactured symbols to the forefront of consciousness, the uprooting of traditional

[34] Simondon, 247.
[35] *"La chute des référentiels."* See Lefebvre, 209ff.

156

languages (for example, of art, music, and literature), and the tendency toward the confusion of formal and ordinary language eliminated the traditional, unreflected distinction between the denotative and referential (contextual) functions of language. In the new universal semiotic of technological experience, in which "form and content, if they still exist, are on the same level," language and images became *the* referential wherein all aspects of action and meaning became intertranslatable subsystems. Owing to the penetration of everyday life by technology, all sectors of the former become intertranslatable and saturated with meanings derived from relation to other sectors, so that the new referential is what Henri Lefebvre has called *quotidienneté,* quotidianity or everydayness.[36] This referential requires for its comprehension what Barthes calls a "total ideological description, common to all the systems of a simple synchronicity."[37]

One of the central features of this semiotic system, a feature that is both essential to its operation and constitutive of the specific experience of one-dimensional society, is the overcoming of the distinction between conscious and unconscious, and the externalization of the unconscious. Conscious and unconscious become interrelated symbolic systems that, although on different levels, derive their meanings from the same sources. This is the meaning of psychoanalysis. For thousands of years, the dream had stood at the frontier between two worlds: no-one knew what was

[36] In his book *La Vie Quotidienne* Lefebvre nowhere provides a univocal definition of this concept. In the present context its most important aspects are the disappearance of meanings that transcend daily life and justify it, the permeation of the details of life by the forms of the social system, the establishment of daily life as the social locus of feedback in the system, and the awareness that there is nothing more than daily life.

[37] Barthes, 119.

157

across the frontier, but the existence of the frontier itself gave a precise sense to the conception of reality as everything on this side. Within the universal semiotic of technological experience, psychoanalysis crossed the frontier. The dream became translatable. The result was not just finding out what was on the other side but finding out that the other side was already here, that the rationalization of the unconscious illuminated the irrationality of the conscious. The continuity established between the two mediated their contents and structures with each other. The unconscious now exists as the continually moving limit of the process of translation, a process in which the language into which we translate changes as it incorporates what was previously not formulated within it. Simultaneously, through technology and its link to art and sensation, "our unconscious system is in the course of reconstructing itself in bits and pieces outside us."[38] Technology breaks down the unconscious, organizes it, and recombines it in forms that structure the previously "external" world. We shall see below how modern design facilitates this activity, which is propelled both by the dialectic of consumption, through which commodities are adapted to ever deeper levels of the consumers' desires and fantasies while the latter are increasingly molded by industry, and by the mere fact of the system's self-regulation within a framework which has not been consciously chosen. To understand this mechanism we must first investigate the relations of technology to art, biology, and the senses.

Traditionally the dichotomies of two-dimensional civilization came to expression in the separation of the realms of the useful and the beautiful in such a way that aesthetic experience was the stimulus to and the token of the experi-

[38] Simonis, 334.

ence of critically transcending the realm of necessity and function. Art seemed to provide an immediate sensuous experience of what lay (metaphysically or historically) beyond the world of unfreedom. This manifested itself at the poles of experience: in the connection of the beautiful with the divine (as in Plato) and morality (in Kant), and the resistance of sensuality to the reality-principle in ordinary life, expressed in the countless taboos that were intended to control it. This capacity of art derived, as we have seen, from its ability to synthesize the universal and the particular, form and content, in a manner that was impossible in other realms of experience, owing to the conflict between form and content derived from the backward state of technical development. From this conflict came as well the downgrading of the senses as sources of knowledge. At the height of industrial civilization, however, the senses began to empower themselves of the functional world, while they themselves were disempowered by technicity. The technical world began its evolution toward being the object, aim, and source of aesthetic experience.

We see that where the engineer has worked purposefully without any aesthetic intentions and no artist has intervened in the work, a pure and 100% modern beauty was attained with new materials. The machine was produced not as a spectacle but for use; nevertheless, looking at a factory in operation is a dizzying modern theatre.[39]

In the moment when we attain a uniform, functional perfection, we also automatically arrive at beauty.[40]

The more perfect a machine is, the more beautiful it becomes.[41]

---

[39] Karel Teige, *Liquidierung der Kunst* (Frankfurt am Main: Suhrkamp, 1968), 66.
[40] *Ibid.*, 67.
[41] *Ibid.*, 68.

The integral aesthetic organization of the machine becomes, with the neotechnic economy, the final step in ensuring its efficiency.[42]

From these words we can see that aesthetic utopia, what Marcuse calls "sensuous rationality," is built into the logic of technological development itself. According to Karel Teige, it is the mechanical world that makes possible the "poetry of the senses."[43] But the latter is not the language of utopia; however corrupted, it is the language of the world in which we live.

The import of the fusion of beauty and function, art and industry, the senses and the machine, is to override the distinction between the senses and their objects, inside and outside. The joint mediations of the relations man-nature and sensuousness-technology has made technology a form of experience (including sense experience) and experience a form of technology. Just as the technical world and the world of commodities and objects become anthropomorphic, so the human world becomes technomorphic. This follows from the neotechnic reciprocal adaptation of technology and biology: "instead of mechanism forming a pattern for life, living organisms began to form a pattern for mechanism."[44] This adaptation itself occurs in the realm of technical action:

The permanent agreement between physical realities and the mathematical instruments used to describe them . . . is not simply . . . that of a language with designated objects (for it is not the habit of languages to tell in advance the events that they describe) but that of human operations with object-operators, thus a harmony between the particular operator (or maker of multiple operations) that man is in his body and mind, and

42 Mumford, 253.
43 "Manifest des Poetismus" (Manifesto of Poetism) in *op. cit.*
44 Mumford, 216.

the innumerable operators that are physical objects at all levels: there is here thus . . . the best example of known biological adaptations (that is, physico-chemical and cognitive at the same time).[45]

It must be emphasized, however, that although the adaptation of technology and biology is two-way, the technological always predominates, both because the system as a whole is technological and because the adaptation of technology to biology occurs only in the service of technological ends. For within the system the needs of life are not ends but only means for the expansion of the system. We shall see below that within technological experience, the relationship of art and needs to technology can be reversed; it is the point at which freedom can enter the system.

How does the synthesis of art and technology affect the process of semiotization? Primarily by means of modern design, which becomes the form of the universal technological experience. The evolution of modern design is an essential component of the process of one-dimensionality, and indeed serves as an index of the latter's temporal development, since it derives from the machine process the forms for creating a total (totalitarian) environment in which technological experience defines and closes the experiential and aesthetic universe. As Pevsner writes of Gropius' architecture,

While in the thirteenth century all lines, functional though they were, served the one artistic purpose of pointing heavenwards to a goal beyond this world, and walls were made translucent to carry the transcendental magic of saintly figures rendered in colored glass, the glass walls are now clear and without mystery, the steel frame is hard, and its expression discourages all other-worldly speculation. It is the creative energy of this world in which we live and work and which we want to master, a world

[45] Piaget, *Le Structuralisme,* 36.

161

of science and technique, of speed and danger, of hard struggles and no personal security, that is glorified in Gropius' architecture.[46]

The role of modern design as the form of the universal semiotic of technological experience derives from the predominance of the optic sense and the attendant significance of visual "releasers" in human sign systems, coupled with the increase in the volume and intensity of visual signs and symbols brought about by technology. This makes possible the manipulation of response and experience through modulations of the visual sphere, given the innate human tendency toward the mimic exaggeration of optically effective motions:

That is, the optically effective components [of such motions] are underlined and overemphasized to the point of grotesqueness, very frequently through the development of form and color characteristics that promote optical effects.[47]

Modern design makes use of this in its analysis and synthesis of the world, in which the human perceptual field, nature, and the technical sphere are broken down into their basic components and laws and then recomposed according to the principle of the identity of art and function:

A visual representation of nature can be vital in human experience only if it becomes a nature form itself by reaching an organic quality, a plastic unity.[48]

This is precisely what the art of the past hundred years has been working toward and has achieved. The individual as an organic whole, whose vital faculties were previously

[46] Nikolaus Pevsner, *Pioneers of Modern Design* (New York: Museum of Modern Art, 1949), 135.
[47] Gyorgy Kepes, *Language of Vision* (Chicago: Theobald, 1959), 43.
[48] *Ibid.*, 67.

162

excluded from the world of productive forces and production relations, is now integrated into them through his very acts of perception:

To perceive a visual image implies the beholder's participation in a process of organization. The experience of an image is thus a creative act of integration. Its essential characteristic is formed into an organic whole.[49]

This "organic" whole derives its very organic quality from technology, from the planned, scientific organization of the visual field. Life and technology are identical; nevertheless, technology has the upper hand.

There are several ways in which these properties of modern design enter into the constitution of the universal semiotic of technological experience. First, they contribute to the externalization of the unconscious. It was the analysis of motion that finally made possible this externalization and thus the stabilization of a system in which "conscious" and "unconscious" are homogenized and levelled down to a plane which is not located "in the mind" but everywhere. This analysis of motion, as Siegfried Giedion has pointed out, occurred at the same time in art and in scientific management.

First, movement is dissected into separate phases so that the forms appear side by side or overlapping. This occurs around 1910. The second state makes the *form* of movement into an object of expression. Scientific management does this for purposes of analysis. In art, calligraphic forms are endowed with the power of symbols. This occurs around 1920. The development continues into a third stage, of which we know only the beginning. During the thirties motion forms increasingly become a pictorial language to express psychic content.[50]

[49] *Ibid.*, 13.
[50] Siegfried Giedion, *Mechanization Takes Command* (New York: Norton, 1969), 106.

The construction of the real world can then directly realize unconscious contents in objects and images whose relations become subject to the logic of the unconscious, corrected by the exigencies of the self-regulating technical structure, itself subject to political imperatives. The logic of fantasy and that of reality become mutually adapted.

With the collapse of the traditional institutional supports of taboos and social controls and the transposition of social-ization functions to mass media and the communication system, the institutional rituals, patterns, and compromises in which social conflicts were previously stabilized are now translated into relations of signs and objects:

So does [man] organize the chaos of his psychological space, by forming visual images of his desires, temporary equilibriums in the perpetual conflicts of pleasure and reality; impulses and social taboos.[51]

This translation is facilitated by the integration of all modes of experience and all sides of human nature into the system of design. For if

art is a sensuous form of consciousness, an important instrument in the conquest of nature, and representation is the creative assimilation of nature,[52]

then the nature of man is one of the objects of conquest, and it is through his senses that he is conquered. This is a strong motive in the sensualization of culture:

There is a common structural basis of all kinds of sensations . . . The sensations may call forth intensive emotional response, without rising into consciousness. Painters, musicians, poets, and scientists, aware of the significance and creative potentialities

[51] Kepes, 194.
[52] *Ibid.*, 109.

164

inherent in this structural correspondence, searched and worked for a creative control, for a synchronization of the senses.[53]

This fusion of the senses and technology means that sensuality cannot provide a critique of technology.

Second, both the unconscious and political imperatives, expressed in the language of design, shape the overall environment. For

thanks to the new treatment of glass and steel, the usual hard separation of exterior and interior is annihilated. Light and air can pass freely through the walls so that the closed-in space is no longer different in essence from the great universe of space outside.[54]

This result of modern architecture is decisive in eliminating the experience of the opposition of man and nature, consciousness and being. Instead of humanly organized space existing as an enclave within nature, all of nature is continuous with and therefore relativized with regard to humanly organized space, so that architects and planners can, so to speak, design the entire spatially experienceable universe. This undoubtedly contributes to the genesis of the specific form of the negative experience of one-dimensional man described thus by Sartre:

Lucid, immobile, deserted, consciousness is posed between the walls: it perpetuates itself. No-one inhabits it any longer. Just now someone still said *me,* said *my* consciousness. Who? Outside there were talking streets, with known colors and odors. There remain anonymous walls, an anonymous consciousness. Here is what there is: walls, and between the walls, a little transparency, alive and impersonal. Consciousness exists like a tree, like a blade of grass. It dozes, it is bored.[55]

[53] Ibid., 167. See also Teige, *loc. cit.*
[54] Pevsner, 132.
[55] Jean-Paul Sartre, *La Nausée* (Paris: Gallimard, 1962), 239.

Third, through the visual medium the unconscious and technological rationality, with the structures of domination and repression they incorporate, are built into the fabric of daily life and constitute the field of quotidianity. The extension of mechanization to all areas of life, such as the household and the bathroom, integrates the most private and individual parts of life into the semiotic system, from which they derive their meaning and structure: this goes hand in hand with the integration of the spheres of labor and leisure.[56] Buildings, furniture, advertisements, clothes, facial expressions, and fantasies become increasingly inter-adapted; their meanings refer to each other and become homogenized. The individual, whether person or object, is de-individualized through technological analysis and synthesis, and becomes no more than a unit or locus in a field of total design whose laws determine his or its meaning and our reaction. By means of the science of design, of visual relations, the person or thing is decomposed into elements of line, shape, light, and color, which are then reformed according to supra-individual patterns of meaning and their connotations, and it is in accordance with these patterns that we respond to it or him. One example of this is the development of furniture in the twentieth century, which is a "furniture of *types,* not of individual pieces."[57] The problem of furniture design within the framework of the spatial ideas of the new architecture was not "designing single pieces or even complete suites of furniture." Instead, the room and its contents "were felt as a single entity."[58] In turn, the

[56] On the mechanization of the household and bathroom, see parts 6 and 7 of Giedion, *op. cit.* The reciprocal adaptation of technology and the human body can be observed in an ideal manner in Alexander Kira's book *The Bathroom: criteria for design* (New York: Bantam, 1967).

[57] Giedion, 9.

[58] *Ibid.,* 484.

166

room was felt as part of the building, and the latter as part of the total spatial conception of modern design. Furniture was dissected into its elements, into a "system of struts and planes."[59] With this analysis completed, it became possible to synthesize the basic elements to fit a given spatial context:

The architects first created the surrounding spaces, and then, from the same spatial feeling, their furniture. The types are conceived in functional terms.[60]

The same subordination of the individual is carried out in the personal world by two qualities of the technical object: its communicative function and the form of this function. We saw above that the technical object is communication *per se* as a transindividual relation. This communication not only links individuals, it also destroys them. For the individual, in order to assimilate the information provided by the object, must adapt his perceptual, cognitive, and practical modes to it. A network is established in which all individuals are intentionally related to one another *a priori* through the technical object: no longer, however, as subjects in the traditional sense, but as operational units connected according to "field" laws of the system in which persons, their parts, objects, and signs all function indifferently as units. This transindividual relation is the technical foundation of the unconscious as the level on which the communication acts of the universal semiotic of technological experience take place:

The opposition between me and the other [is] surmounted on a terrain that is also the one where the objective and the subjective meet, namely the unconscious,[61]

[59] *Ibid.*, 485.
[60] *Ibid.*, 508.
[61] Claude Lévi-Strauss, quoted in Simonis.

an unconscious that is no longer personal or internal but collective and external.

The form of the communicative function is the *"regard sur l'objet technique,"* the gaze at the technical object:

The gaze at the technical object, a passive gaze, attentive only to functioning, interested only in structure (disassembling and re-assembling), fascinated by that spectacle without background, complete in its transparent surface, this gaze becomes the prototype of the social act.[62]

This gaze becomes the model especially of the sexual relation in one-dimensional society, in its assimilation of the sexual object with the machine; its identification of the sexual gaze with the passive masturbation fantasy and the cool gaze at television and advertising; in its projection of the fantasies of mechanical power onto the sexual object, with consequent masochism; and in its over-all Midas-like reification of the other and the self so that interpenetration and real gratification become impossible. Accordingly, the sexual object is programmed with planned obsolescence, to be consumed and replaced. The *regard sur l'objet technique* as the predominant sexual mode is expressed in the universal symbol of sunglasses, which permit both the gaze at and identification with the technical object. The elevation of the technical object to the model sexual object propagates a universal form of sexual fantasy that is frustrating and self-perpetuating because it is unrealizable, namely, the desire to have sexual experience in which one is not there as a subject, that is, with structures of intersubjectivity, responsibility, and temporality, but only as an object, in a moment of transparency in which two objects collide. In other words, the ideal is to be transfigured into no more than a sign in the system. As Walter Benjamin wrote of the

[62] Lefebvre, 96.

public's identification with movie stars, "the public only empathizes with the movie star by empathizing with the apparatus."[63]

Sexuality is only prototypical for the range of action and experience taken over by the gaze at the technical object. In *The Image,* Daniel Boorstin has described how today's social and cultural life functions as a totality of pseudo-events, events created by and for the need to consume them: from political events to personal experience.[64] Ernest Schachtel has analyzed the way in which

experience increasingly assumes the form of the cliché under which it will be recalled because this cliché is what conventionally is remembered by others. This is not the remembered situation itself, but the words which are customarily used to indicate this situation and the reactions which it is supposed to evoke.[65]

Benjamin has also pointed out how the film has modified optical perception of daily life to the point where our normal perception of the world is perception mediated by the camera.[66]

What emerges from all of this is both the notion of the schematization of experience according to laws of the semiotic system and the need for a new conception of reality. Experience becomes schematized when its internal structure, its patterns of symbols and their relation to affects, are formalized and become operational. When unconscious psychic meanings can be translated into systems of visual signs, then "reality" becomes a dream, for every-

[63] "Das Kunstwerk im Zeitalter seiner technischen Reproduzierbarkeit" (The Art Work in the Era of its Technical Reproducibility), *Illuminationen* (Frankfurt am Main: Suhrkamp, 1961), 161.

[64] New York: Harper, 1964.

[65] "On Memory and Childhood Amnesia," *Metamorphosis* (New York: Basic Books, 1959), 288.

[66] Benjamin, 168ff.

169

thing in it has meaning according to objectified unconscious laws. The universal semiotic of technological experience makes possible the "resolution of the two states, dream and reality, into a sort of absolute reality."[67] In this absolute reality, in which objects and images are saturated with meaning, we carry out somnambulistic actions in a dream world in which our desires, conflicts, and fantasies are condensed and displaced. The difference between our reactions to a sports car and a passenger car has little to do with their functions, which are usually identical, or their pure aesthetic value. Rather we react to their designs, in which different meanings and psychic values (power, sex, spectacularity) have been visually incorporated, as in streamlining, and to meanings allocated by connotative systems.[68] In fact, we do not have reactions or undertake actions. For our actions are only means through which the transformational laws of the system are carried out.

In what way is this system a system of political domination? In the immediate sense, the patterns of meaning within the universal semiotic of technological experience are constituted not merely by the evolution of technology alone, but by social interests of domination. When we read that

advertising art, unhandicapped by traditional considerations, was free to develop a visual representation in which every figure is pictured in the perspective which gives the strongest emphasis to its connectedness in a meaning,[69]

we understand that the meaning-organization is shaped by a manipulative interest, and that this interest affects the person, since the manipulation takes place within "his" mind, that is, its total content of symbols and images. In

[67] André Breton, quoted in Kepes, 210.
[68] A semiological study of the automobile can be found in Lefebvre, 191–198.
[69] Kepes, 194.

addition, whole subsystems of meaning are manipulated systems or languages, referred to by Barthes as "logo-techniques," that is, languages elaborated not by the speaking masses, but by decision groups, for example technocracies.[70] The "logo-technique" has truly arbitrary signs, because it is fabricated by unilateral decision. A considerable part of today's total semiotic system is formed in this way.

More generally, the political character and function of technology, as Jürgen Habermas has argued, operates through the integration of symbolically mediated interaction and purposively rational action. That is, patterns of social interaction, which are based on social norms and reciprocity and are the basis of *praxis* and politics, become invisible or lost in patterns of instrumental and strategic action based on technical rules and a context-free formalized language.[71] This is made possible by the general process of technological semiotization and its occurrence within a pre-given political framework. The political system adapted to change through increased bureaucratization and the extension of formal rationality at the same time that scientific technology and communications transformed both the production process and daily life into purposively rational patterns. In this way, communicative relations can be limited by social norms of authority and inequality that manifest themselves as structures of rational, technical authority from which reciprocity is eliminated and in which feedback occurs only as data for control, not as a form of intersubjectivity. Conversely, the extension of technical rationality is itself limited when it runs up against political priorities: the self-regulation of technical systems is limited

[70] Barthes, 103.
[71] Habermas, "Technik und Wissenschaft als 'Ideologie,'" *Technik und Wissenschaft,* 81ff.

or directed by the unquestionable rules of the game. Political meanings are distorted and become "unconscious" through displacement. But, in the last analysis, the political character of the system derives from the mere acceptance of its self-regulation. Through the absorption of subjectivity into objectivity, political domination operates through the universal semiotic of technological experience by means of the mere elimination of choice and the consciousness of choice.

Is this depiction of one-dimensionality not even more "pessimistic" than Marcuse's is alleged to be? Does the universal semiotic of technology so smoothly absorb everything into itself that it is completely self-regulating? If all of human experience is reduced to technology, can technology be used for ends beyond itself? Does one-dimensionality not have a dialectic of its own? What forms of praxis does it make even thinkable, let alone feasible?

One-dimensionality does have its own dialectic, its own determinate negation both as a form of experience and a form of praxis. But, like all dialectical processes, the determinate negation of one-dimensionality is generated by and within the latter. We can only get beyond the one-dimensional world as we know it if we first accept it as real, as an historically irreversible stage, which we must regard as inevitable. Indeed I should like to borrow an originally theological image, so frequent in the philosophy of history and present even in Marxism, and argue that one-dimensionality is an educational phase in the history of the human species. This does not mean that we have any guarantee that we can get out of its repressive features: the very notion of such a guarantee is part of the system of domination. But the real thrust even of such a critique of one-dimensionality as Marcuse's is that this is so: it is the pacification of the world through technology, the synthesis

172

of subjectivity and objectivity, of freedom and necessity, of art and industry that makes possible the pacification of social, human, erotic, and aesthetic existence. Violette Morin has stated this explicitly with regard to Eros. According to her, contemporary eroticism, that is, what Marcuse calls repressive desublimation, is a "great historical victory" of capitalistic, consumption-oriented society, because the latter has domesticated sexuality and eroticism, eliminating the archaic terror, fear, and mystery with which they have been bound up.[72] Despite the hypersanguinity and oversimplification of this statement, it expresses a truth. But in this abstract form, both Miss Morin's notion and the concept of repressive desublimation are useless for practice, because they do not provide any criteria for distinguishing between the progressive and regressive features of one-dimensional civilization, or, better stated, for intervening in this civilization in order to crystallize and direct its progressive, negative, and human potentialities. For this we need to examine the dialectic of one-dimensionality.

In the dialectic of one-dimensionality, the type of contradiction that prevailed in two-dimensional civilization has been overcome or resolved, whether in a "good" or "bad" way. The traditional dialectic, including Marx's, presupposed the dichotomy of the two dimensions of form and matter, universal and particular, and the other characteristic vertical distinctions. In the universal semiotic of technological experience, contradictions have become horizontal.

[72] Violette Morin and Joseph Majault, *Un Mythe Moderne: L'Érotisme* (Paris: Casterman, 1964), 69. Analogously, Tom Nairn has argued in his brilliant and essential essay on the causes of the French revolution of 1968 that the unification and socialization of consciousness under advanced capitalism is a prerequisite of the new revolution and not merely a form of brainwashing. See Angelo Quattrocchi and Tom Nairn, *The Beginning of the End: France, May 1968* (London: Panther, 1968).

This affects crucially the "antagonistic" character of contradictions *per se*. In an antagonistic contradiction, one side has an explosive character: affirming it disintegrates the identity of which it is a part. If the contradiction is *aufgehoben* or overcome, then this side is no longer explosive, for it is already thoroughly mediated with its opposite. In one-dimensional society, the latter form of contradiction becomes basic. Under capitalism as well as socialism, all contradictions are non-antagonistic. That is why the traditionally explosive elements of civilization, the lower class, the individual, sensuality, and so forth are no longer revolutionary by nature: not because they are bought off, manipulated, repressed, but because they are mediated with, part and parcel of, their antithesis. They are part of a system of rules in which everything implies everything else, in which the dissolution of individuals into relations means that the ground to stand on is dispersed horizontally throughout the system.

The needs and values that traditionally opposed domination are still present. Suffering, resistance to authority, perception of exploitation have not been occluded out of the universe. Rather they have been distorted and molded in technical forms by political imperatives, mixed, decomposed and analyzed, resynthesized, and distributed throughout experience. The system is in imperfect equilibrium, because in the process of mediation in nature and society, new and even negative elements continually appear. But they are immediately reduced to and incorporated within the system, taking on the structure dictated by the political imperatives. The system seems to change continually through innovation and rearrangement. For the "value" of any component derives from the "reciprocal situation of the pieces of the language"; the content of the sign is "less important than that which surrounds it in the

174

other signs."[73] Thus the introduction of a new element changes the value of all other elements. However, although this accounts for the experience of continual novelty, it also ensures the subordination of change to the regular laws of the system. Thus meanings of the semiotic system may connote domination and oppression, but in a mystified, mystifying, and continually shifting way that makes it difficult to get hold of them, make sense of them, develop them, and turn them into praxis. Understanding the dialectic of one-dimensionality means abandoning the search for a fixed, definite locus of negativity "outside" the system. Instead we must learn to understand it as a way of translating the universal semiotic of technological experience in a way that "collects" negativity from its dispersion throughout the system and uses it to restructure the system from within by reversing the relations of already existing imperatives. This demands a new form of experience, a new comprehension of the relationship between subjectivity and objectivity, and a new practice.

Radicalism presupposes "negative experience." The negative experience of early capitalism was the proletarian experience of absolute need and oppression, the experience of privation. It was this experience that was supposed to be transformed into revolutionary class-consciousness. One-dimensionality creates its own specific form of immediate negative experience which is the experience best articulated in such writers as Kafka and Sartre: absurdity, nausea, superfluity, meaninglessness, schizophrenia, being lost in existence. Earlier I quoted Sartre's *La Nausée* in this connection. Consciousness is "anonymous," is a "little transparency, alive and impersonal. Consciousness exists like a tree . . . It dozes, it is bored." Elsewhere in the same work, we read,

[73] Ferdinand de Saussure, quoted in Barthes, 128.

I let myself plop down on the bench, dazed, stunned by this profusion of beings without origin: hatching and blooming everywhere. My ears buzzed with existence, my very flesh palpitated and opened up, abandoned itself to the universal budding, it was repugnant. "But why," I thought, "why so many existences, since they are all alike."[74]

And, in another passage,

Extra [*de trop*], the chestnut tree, opposite me there a bit to the left . . . and *I . . . I too was extra* . . . I dreamed vaguely of doing away with myself, to annihilate at least one of these superfluous existences. But my death itself would have been extra.[75]

This is the experience of man lost in the world, distributed through the world. He no longer *confronts* it, for he and and the manifold of the world have been reduced to superfluous, identical existence. Consciousness is no longer either personal or subjective. Instead it is anonymous, placed between the walls. Man as an impersonal, anonymous, transparency is man translated into the universal semiotic of technological experience. In the world of pure existence there is no negation; rather, negation, like death, is just another existence, every one of which is, in its resemblance to the others, *de trop*. The experience of being *de trop* is an historically new form of negative experience, namely, existence as a set of contradictory relations in the interior of objects and images.

This negative experience is the starting point for radical theory and practice. And, desperate as this situation seems, it is at the same time ripe for change. For the integration of subjectivity and objectivity, freedom and necessity, art and technology implied in current negative experience contains the basis not only for total control and manipulation

[74] Sartre, 188.
[75] *Ibid.*, 182.

under imperatives of political domination but for total liberation under the imperatives of freedom. The synthesis of art, life, and the machine is the basis not only of mass culture and repressive desublimation, but also of sensuous rationality. Indeed, this is its danger. The new sensibility, the aesthetic-erotic morality of which Marcuse writes is itself the product of technology. And as technological, aesthetic-erotic morality, it is in continual danger of remaining within the purely technological sphere. Thus the new sensibility can be radical only if it is subject to the imperative of a new *subjectivity,* a subjectivity *within* objectivity.

In the last three centuries of two-dimensional civilization, from which we inherit our philosophical tradition, the problem of freedom was thought out in terms of the relation between subject and object, freedom and necessity, free will and causality. The classical formulation of this is in Kant's theory of the distinction of the phenomenal self, subject to the laws of causality, from the noumenal self, capable of free will. Now this dichotomy is only a reflection of the relation of form and content before technological mediation has "discovered the interiority of the relation." Technology, by discovering it, overcomes the antinomy of freedom and causality.

The technical object, thought and constructed by man, does not limit itself to creating a mediation between man and nature; it is a stable mixture of the human and the natural, it contains the properties of both the human and the natural within it; it gives its human content a structure similar to that of natural objects, and permits the insertion of this human reality into the world of natural causes and effects. . . . A convertibility of the human into the natural and of the natural into the human institutes itself by means of technical schematism.[76]

[76] Simondon, 245.

This means that in one-dimensional civilization the translation of human needs into the objective world is to be effected not by a leap between two realms but by a reorientation within a single one. It is this technological dissolution of the Kantian antinomy that lies at the root of the philosophy of life and existentialist philosophy that emerged during the period of the emergence and stabilization of one-dimensional civilization. Bergson's critique of Kant's theory of freedom as a necessary consequence of the latter's erroneous theory of time reflects the replacement of the mechanical model of the paleotechnic period, in which time is spatialized, by the model of the neotechnic period, in which "living organisms began to form a pattern for mechanism." Reflection on life history reveals moments "when we made some serious decision, moments unique of their kind, which will never be repeated."[77] These decisions are not subjective or objective, but both at once. They are crystallizations of choice within an ongoing process of the universal semiotic of technological experience, in which the system is immanently transcended. The process of reflection and the awareness of freedom enable the new sensibility to shape technology in the direction of liberation.

Translation and choice: these are the two keys to the development of radical practice. Translation means deciphering the total semiotic system, formulating the various subsystems of meaning on a level where experience becomes meaningful and thereby subject to choice.[78] What is not meaningfully experienced cannot be the basis of radical, intentional social change. Where the relationship of the different types of experience is not experienced as a unity, then meaning is impossible, and if a vital modality of ex-

[77] Henri Bergson, *Time and Free Will* (New York: Harper, 1960), 239.

[78] On the contribution to decision and action of the interpretation of meaning see Fingarette, especially Chapter 1.

perience is missing, then meaningful unity cannot be sustained. Either it is recovered by an energetic labor of mediation, reflection, or action, or it disappears as a possible component of meaningful experience. The current moment of world-history is one in which experience is being extensively and intensively liberated, that is, made more conscious, formulated, and capable of communication and mediation. At the same time experience is being radically simplified, conventionalized, and mystified. Everyday life has become the medium of experience, and it is only through its formulation that intervention is possible. And it pertains to the nature of one-dimensionality that formulation and analysis go over into practice. Henri Lefebvre writes of socio-analysis as a science that would

unveil [the] relations implicated in quotidianity, but implicit and veiled in the heart of daily life. . . . It supposes intervention in the existing situation, the quotidianity of a group. Socio-analytic intervention *dissociates* the aspects of the quotidian situation, mixed with false obviousness, in a single place and time. It *associates* them with experiences that were previously external. It then proceeds by induction and transduction.[79]

Here we have come to the idea of a psychoanalysis of the external world, which follows logically from the fact of the integration of the conscious and the unconscious and the latter's externalization. Just as personal psychoanalysis involves translation of the patient's private language into a language shared by the patient and analyst, so the psychoanalysis of the external world involves translating the meanings concealed in the universal semiotic of technological experience into the language of a social group oriented toward extension of the limits of comprehension and choice. Since each individual's private language and un-

[79] Lefebvre, 345.

conscious exist "out there" in the world of everyday life, the psychoanalysis and socioanalysis of the external world must be integrated with psychoanalysis of the internal world.

As a method of political praxis, such analysis must have as a primary goal reconstitution of the individual and his differentiation from the group.[80] One of the chief contributions of traditional forms of socialist organizations to perpetuating the system of one-dimensionality is through their elimination of individuality, which is a prerequisite of praxis even for groups. Praxis, by its very nature, implies an element of personal decision and judgment which cannot be reduced to or accounted for by theory. The latter

offers the specific rules of action as parts of a reasoned whole and without making a decision. The particular execution itself has no theory of its own and can have none. Though applying the theory, it is not simply derivative of it but involves decision based on *judgment:* and there is no science of judgment (as little as there is one of decision), [which, as the faculty of subsuming the particular under the universal,] is necessarily outside science and strictly the bridge between the abstractions of the understanding and the concreteness of life.[81]

Recognizing this, the Greeks treated politics as an extension of ethics. The goal of both was the education of a *character* that would make it possible for the individual to make the appropriate mediation between the particular and the general in concrete life situations. It is the basic characteristic of modern, bourgeois political theory that the goal of politics is the establishment of technical institutions

80 See the paper by Shierry M. Weber in this volume.
81 Hans Jonas, "The Practical Uses of Theory," *Philosophy of the Social Sciences,* ed. Maurice Natanson (New York: Random House, 1963), 130.

that guarantee justice independently of individual action. The individual is discharged of ethical responsibility. He may pursue his instincts or follow the desire for gain or power; regardless, the political system operates efficiently. This theory is the basis of liberalism: Hobbes and Adam Smith are classic examples.[82]

Unfortunately, this bourgeois theory has carried over to much socialist political thinking. Socialism is supposed to replace an existing, technically imperfect system (the anarchy of socialized production) with a technically perfect system (socialism), and the political theory for effecting the change is itself often regarded as a technical doctrine, containing its own criteria of application and accordingly not requiring individual experience and decision. This leads automatically to the dissociation of one's own life from that of the movement, the identification of an institution (the party) with the theory itself, and the abandonment of the principles of liberation in favor of an alibi system in life situations; that is, the technique of revolution defines ethical behavior, so that the sphere of morality is neutralized. I am not morally responsible for an action that does not fall within the field of application for the technique of revolution. Morality will only exist "after the revolution." Meanwhile, why should I be moral? It won't change the system. Such "socialism" must necessarily reproduce one-dimensionality, that is, political domination masked as technical rationality, and is thus a primary enemy of any liberation movement.

The goal of political practice is to extend the community's realm of choice and decision over the entirety of social life in the interest of needs that do not require domi-

[82] This subject is discussed by Jürgen Habermas in "Die klassische Lehre von der Politik in ihrem Verhältnis zur Sozialphilosophie (The Classical Doctrine of Politics in Its Relation to Social Philosophy), *Theorie und Praxis* (Neuwied: Luchterhand, 1963).

nation. This can only be done through a dialectical process of communication that has the following features. First, in seeking to reverse the imperatives of the system and let subjectivity predominate over, although remaining within objectivity, it must begin with those areas of choice, decision, and freedom which individuals experience as such, heighten experience of the difference between these areas and those in which there is no choice, show that areas of life that are accepted as pre-given represent choices among alternatives, and use imagination and education to project means of opening these self-regulating areas to choice. Second, this process must mediate between individual and group needs and clarify the areas of congruence and difference. The solidarity necessary for political practice requires identity of essential individual needs, whose individuality must be actively experienced. Yet these needs can only be fully experienced in the process of communication. Third, the personal and interpersonal realms will and must continue to persist, but the boundary between them is constantly shifting. The process of communication raises previously personal experience to the interpersonal level. In so doing, it makes possible individual awareness of new aspects of personal experience that could not even be perceived before the process of communication. Much of what appeared to be personal turns out to be impersonal; at the same time, what is really personal becomes visible as a field of force and synthesis amidst the more impersonal forces of the universal semiotic. The supposed antithesis of personal and political liberation is a sign of the immaturity of the radical movement and its subordination to one-dimensionality. Fourth, it is through the process of semiotic translation and interpersonal communication in the interest of freedom that negativity is "recollected" from its dispersion into a point from which choice can be exerted, choice that reverses the relation of art and life on the one hand to technology on the other. Binswanger has explained psychosis as a form of resignation, "a resignation that takes the form of a retreat from *Dasein's* [human existence's] own decision, the complete renunciation of the *Dasein's* own ability to decide and, with this, the complete *self*-surrender to the power of others."[83] The automatic operation of one-dimensionality generates this resignation. Radical practice must attempt to undo it.

It will be clear by this time that this sketch of one-dimensionality, while indebted to the work of Marcuse, also implies a critique of it. For reasons of space I cannot undertake such a critique here. But I should like to indicate the points on which it would concentrate. They are, first, the contradiction between regarding one-dimensionality as a "perversion" of two-dimensionality and regarding it as a necessary stage of technological rationality; second, the relation of the realms of subjectivity, freedom, beauty, and play on the one hand, and objectivity, necessity, utility, and labor on the other, and the question of whether their integration takes place prior to, during, or after the transition from capitalist or one-dimensional to socialist society: third, the relation between idealism and materialism and its corollary, the question of Freudian theory, that is, of a naturalistic psychology; and finally, the problem of negation. I shall elaborate briefly.

First, Marcuse's theory of one-dimensionality tends to take the structure of two-dimensional civilization as "normal," as an absolute standpoint from which one-dimensionality appears as a "repression" of two-dimensionality which, when undone, will return everything to its

[83] Ludwig Binswanger, "Introduction to *Schizophrenie," Being-in-the-World: Selected Papers of Ludwig Binswanger,* translated and edited by Jacob Needleman (New York: Harper, 1967), 263.

prior state. This conception is made explicit in an essay written in 1933.[84] It is worth mentioning in this connection that Marcuse introduced the concept of one-dimensionality (and its relation to two-dimensionality) prior to his "revision" of Marxist theory and long before that experience of post-war American mass consumer society to which so many critics and commentators have attributed his notion of one-dimensional man, for it appears in three works published in the early 1930's.[85] This conception of two-dimensionality as normal is incompatible with many of Marcuse's concepts, such as those of the new sensibility and of sensuous rationality.

Second, Marcuse implies in different contexts that the integration of the two dimensions takes place at different historical stages. It is the nature of technological rationality, as he describes it, to integrate them in contemporary society. Yet he still speaks of them as separate realms that need to be united. I think it makes more sense to speak of different modes of their integration in these two historical stages.

Third, there are strong idealist as well as materialist impulses in Marcuse's thought. The greatness of his achievement is undoubtedly linked to his absorption and synthesis of these two impulses. It was his idealist background that made him sensitive to the problem of one-dimensionality as reification of consciousness, while his materialist studies concretized one-dimensionality in terms of socio-historical structures. Yet in turning from idealism to materialism, Marcuse overreacted, adopting a natural-

[84] "Über die philosophischen Grundlagen des wirtschaftswissenschaftlichen Arbeitsbegriffs," reprinted in Herbert Marcuse, *Kultur und Gesellschaft II* (Frankfurt am Main: Suhrkamp, 1965); see esp. 47.
[85] "Über die philosophischen Grundlagen," *Hegels Ontologie und die Grundlegung einer Theorie der Geschichtlichkeit* (Frankfurt am Main: Klostermann, 1932), and "Zum Begriff des Wesens," available in English as "The Concept of Essence," in Herbert Marcuse, *Negations,* with translations by Jeremy J. Shapiro (Boston: Beacon, 1968).

istic psychology, that of Freud, whose inattention to the structure of subjectivity as well as his biological reductionism are inappropriate for grasping the problem of one-dimensionality. Freud's metapsychology has two fundamental weaknesses: the reduction of qualitative psychic phenomena to quantitative relations of psychic energy, and the parallel reduction of structures of subjectivity to objects, such as the ego, the superego, and the id. Both of these reductions are themselves reflections of the technological mentality and are thus poor weapons for criticizing it.

Finally, Marcuse's retention of the two-dimensional model combined with the biological trend of Freudian theory lead him to look for forces of negation outside the very system which he has shown to have no outside.[86] This promotes fluctuation between pessimism about the lack of a revolutionary agent and optimism that sometimes leads to an almost uncritical identification with existing antiauthoritarian forces. Marcuse has written that the term "outside" is metaphorical and really refers to an internal qualitative difference.[87] Such a difference, however, is better expressed as a new form of subjectivity than as a biological need.

These criticisms in no way imply that Marcuse's work has become either obsolete or irrelevant. On the contrary. The greatness of theorists can be assessed by means of our need to go back to them in order to understand the problems that we face. Each step in understanding ourselves advances our understanding of them, and vice versa—the so-called hermeneutic circle. It is of the nature of great thought that it is still being thought—by us. The great thinkers caught major problems, tendencies, and potential-

[86] See "Zum Begriff der Negation in der Dialektik," in Herbert Marcuse, *Ideen zu einer kritischen Theorie der Gesellschaft* (Frankfurt am Main: Suhrkamp, 1969), 185–190.
[87] *Ibid.*, 189.

ities in a nuclear state to which we must return to see where we are, but they could see only the explosion, not the ultimate reaches of the liberated particles. The importance and ineluctability of Marcuse's work comes from its nearness to the nuclear problems of our time, such that only through it can we proceed. For it grasps and brings into systematic interconnection all of the social and historical trends that differentiated our era from its predecessor. If Marcuse has become a bestseller and a magical name even for many who have not read him, it is through a dim awareness that the present has left behind the society legitimized or criticized in the cliches of social thought, and that Marcuse has figured out how. His thought is what Brecht termed *"eingreifendes Denken,"* intervening thought:

the dialectic as that classification, ordering, and way of considering the world which, by showing up its revolutionary contradictions, makes intervention possible.[88]

[88] Bertholt Brecht, *Gesammelte Werke* (Frankfurt am Main: Suhrkamp, 1967), 20:170f.

Notes on Contributors

PAUL BREINES (1941) lives in Cambridge, Mass. A graduate student in European history at the University of Wisconsin, he is preparing a dissertation on Georg Lukács and Karl Korsch in the early 1920s and, with his daughter Natasha Breines, is working on a joint theoretical and practical study of the dissolution of paternal authority in late capitalist society.

RUSSELL JACOBY (1945) is a former second-string high school basketball player and, presently, co-editor of the journal *Foul Play.*

WILLIAM LEISS (1939) received graduate degrees in history of ideas and philosophy from Brandeis and University of California at San Diego. He currently teaches courses in social theory at the University of Saskatchewan (Regina), Canada. With John David Ober (see below) and Erica Sherover he is co-contributor to *The Critical Spirit,* the Marcuse Festschrift.

JOHN DAVID OBER (n.d.) received graduate degrees in history of ideas at Brandeis. He has taught at Connecticut College and currently teaches courses in history and social theory at Antioch College.

JEREMY J. SHAPIRO (1940) is co-director of the Center for the Study of Technological Experience at the California Institute of the Arts in Los Angeles. He studied philosophy, sociology, and history at Harvard, Frankfurt-am-Main, and Brandeis, for which he is completing a dissertation on "The End of All Things: The French Revolution as *Eschaton* in Germany." He is the translator of Herbert Marcuse's *Negations* and, with Shierry M. Weber, co-translator of Marcuse's *Five Lectures*.

SHIERRY M. WEBER (1941) is co-director of the Center for the Study of Technological Experience at the California Institute of the Arts. She is active in the women's liberation movement; is finishing a dissertation on the notion of reflection on Kant's aesthetics for a comparative literature degree from Cornell University; has been teaching German and French at Suffolk University; has studied social theory and psychology in Frankfurt-am-Main; and is co-translator of T. W. Adorno's *Prisims* and, with Jeremy J. Shapiro, of Herbert Marcuse's *Five Lectures*.